Gerard Dillon

Irish Peasant Children, oil on canvas, 14"x12", signed, circa 1949.
Exhibited Institute of Contemporary Art, Boston 1950. PC.

Gerard Dillon

AN ILLUSTRATED BIOGRAPHY

Self Portrait with Pierrot and Nude, oil on board, 22" x 18", signed.
Exhibited IELA 1971. The National Gallery of Ireland

Gerard Dillon

AN ILLUSTRATED BIOGRAPHY

JAMES WHITE

WOLFHOUND PRESS

First published 1994 by
WOLFHOUND PRESS Ltd
68 Mountjoy Square
Dublin 1

British Library Cataloguing in Publication Data
White, James
        Gerard Dillon: Illustrated Biography
        I. Title II. Dillon, Gerard
        759.2

        ISBN 0-86327-370-X   Hardback
        ISBN 0-86327-364-5   Limited edition

'In Memory of Gerard Dillon' by Michael Longley on
page 6, is from *Poems 1963 - 1983*, first published in
the *Irish Times*.
'The Black Lake' by John Montague is from *Mount
Eagle* (The Gallery Press, Oldcastle 1988)

Typesetting: Wolfhound Press
Cover and book design: Jan de Fouw
Cover illustration: *The Painter's Dilemma,* oil on
canvas, 48"x48", signed. PC.
Printed in Ireland by Betaprint, Dublin

Acknowledgements

This book could not have been written without the
generous help of the artist's family, Mr and Mrs
Gerard J. Dillon and Mr and Mrs Martin Dillon, and
of his long-standing friends, Madge Connolly, Pino
Saglietti, Rose Brown, Fr. Joe McBrearty, Arthur
Campbell, Phil Rafferty, Dr Maura Mc Quaid, Madge
Campbell, Mr and Mrs Tom Davidson, Alice West,
Noreen Rice, Cyril Murray, Arthur Armstrong,
Richard Kingston, Michael Longley, Mr and Mrs Hal
Rice, Bill Naughton, Joseph Quilty, Louis Le Brocquy,
Pat Scott and Anne Yeats.

The author is most grateful to John Taylor and the
staff of the Taylor Galleries, Dublin, the Director and
staff of the National Gallery of Ireland, the Director
and staff of the Ulster Museum, the Curator and staff
of the Municipal Gallery of Modern Art in Dublin, the
Director and staff of An Chomhairle Ealaíon, the
Director and staff of the Arts Council of Northern
Ireland and all the following who were most
generous of their time in my researches — I have
listed them alphabetically to simplify identification:
Bruce Arnold, Gus Berger, John Boyd, Mr and Mrs
Wesley Boyd, Edward Brady, Tom Caldwell, Mary
Carroll, Michael Carroll, Bob Collins (RTE), Tadhg
Crowley, Most Rev. Dr Daly, Bishop of Derry, Pat
Flavin, Pat Foley, Douglas Gageby, Michael Gorman,
Donal Guilfoyle, Elizabeth Guinness, Peter Harbison,
Patrick Hickey, Bernard Jaffa, Gerard Keenan, John
Kelly, Brian Kennedy, Jim King, Peter Lamb, Adrian
Le Harivel, Solly Lipsitz, Michael Longley, Percy
Lovegrove, Brendan Madden, Peter Murray, Mr and
Mrs Tom McCreanor, Helen McDonnell, Ciaran
McGonigal, Jimmy O'Brien, Teresa O'Donnell, James
O'Driscoll, Letitia Pollard, Maeve Ryan, Dr Frances
Ruane, Martin Sheridan, Theo Snoddy, Terence
Trench.

Finally, I thank my wife for her constant help and for
reading the manuscript so carefully and I dedicate the
book to the memory of my daughter, Catherine, who
died on 16th January 1989 and for whom Gerard had
painted a picture, aware that like her sister and
brothers she loved him and his paintings.

JAMES WHITE

Contents

In Memory of Gerard Dillon

You walked, all of a sudden, through
The rickety gate which opens
To a scatter of curlews,
An acre of watery light; your grave
A dip in the dunes where sand mislays
The sound of the sea, earth over you
Like a low Irish sky; the sun
An electric light bulb clouded
By the sandy tides, sunlight lost
And found, a message in a bottle.

You are a room full of self-portraits,
A face that follows us everywhere;
An ear to the ground listening for
Dead brothers in layers; an eye
Taking in the beautiful predators —
Cats on the windowsill, birds of prey
And, between the diminutive fields,
A dragonfly, wings full of light
Where the road narrows to the last farm.

Christening robes, communion dresses,
The shawls of factory workers,
A blind drawn on the Lower Falls.

Michael Longley

Above: *Memory Pool*, oil on canvas, 36" x 48", signed. Exhibited IELA 1949. GPA Shannon
Facing page; *Three Biblical Figures*, section of the blind in the family house.
Gouache on Holland Blind material, 13" x 12½". Circa 1941

The Black Lake, oil on canvas, 22" x 28", signed. Exhibited Dawson Gallery Dublin, 1957. The Arts Council of Ireland, Dublin.

Preface

The Black Lake

Across the black lake
Two figures row their boat
With slow, leaning strokes.
The grind of their rowlocks
Is rhythmic as a heartbeat.

Seven stooks stand
In a moonwashed field —
Seven pillars of gold —
While beyond, two haystacks
Roped down to the earth.

Three lean cattle munch
The heavy aftergrass, or
Raise their heads towards
A stonewalled corner where
A couple lean from each other.

The moon climbs the hill.
The night brims with light,
A pantry, silent with milk.
The rowers reach the cottage,
The couple do not speak.

John Montague

In writing this biography, I have tried to set out as simply and directly as possible the events of Gerard Dillon's life and family background in the Falls Road area of Belfast. He grew up in the midst of political and religious strife and also with a degree of parent conflict which affected his character and outlook and conditioned his way of life.

I met him in 1942 when his first exhibition took place in The Country Shop in Dublin and I followed his career with interest ever since, reviewing most of his exhibitions. After his death, his sister, Molly wrote and invited me to write this biography and sent me intimate details of his childhood which I recount. Not a single person, of the many I have interviewed, disagreed with the fact that he most strongly reflected the circumstances and conditions which existed in Belfast from his birth in 1916 until he left at the age of 18 in 1934. Of course, life in London changed him and gave him the impetus to develop, but he clung to all his political and religious prejudices with a determination which was more than surprising.

He was indeed a strong character and any kind of compromise seemed foreign to him. He cultivated simplicity and a love of childhood openness and honesty and he was the only artist whom I ever believed was really sincere when he declared that he wanted to paint with a child's directness. On the other hand, he changed his mind in the middle of his life about the importance of learning to draw properly. His mother had found the money to send him to art school, but he left shortly afterwards, because he could not bear having to imitate the line of the teacher when his instinct was to do it his own way. And though in his biography in *Art in Ulster* by John Hewitt, it is stated that he attended the Belfast Art School for three months, I do not record the fact as I was given to understand that although his fees were paid, he did not turn up after the first couple of nights. Such waywardness was typical of him but also made him the kind of unique individualist he became.

His psycho-sexual nature was formed when he was still quite young and, apart from keeping up appearances to please his mother, he gave up the practice of his religion. He also seemed to reject intimate relationships and to grow up in a very private, solitary environment, always living alone or seeking isolation during the periods when he shared quarters with another friend.

As an artist he was late in developing. This was because he had to earn his living as a house painter, or at some such occupation. He handicapped himself by his obtuse refusal to learn from others and his determination to find out for himself by private investigation. In the long run this meant that his style was the more distinctive, although he did not keep most of his early productions and a large proportion of those he did preserve were destroyed by bombing in London in 1942.

The most important development of his life was his discovery of Connemara. Like so many Ulster artists, Paul Henry, Humbert Craig, Frank McKelvey or Charles Lambe for instance, the West of Ireland represented a discovery with no semblance of the place of conflict left behind in the North. On the contrary, to Gerald Dillon, it seemed removed in every way from the Ireland divided — the scene of the political football which had been going on for so long and which finally erupted in 1916 in the Rising and ultimately brought about the division of the country in 1922 leaving those in the Northern six-counties, in spite of their long Celtic tradition, with an allegiance to the Westminster Government and with good economic reasons to preserve this allegiance.

For a nationalist Catholic like Gerard Dillon, living in London and desperately wanting to belong to a Republican nation called Ireland, his birthplace was now British owned and ruled. On top of that, he had chosen to live in Britain. Connemara, with its remoteness, its delightful stonewall fields, mountains, lakes and seacoast and above all islands like Inishlackan where he could cut himself off for a spell and live in a tiny cottage, with no social life to speak of and a boat journey away from barracks, church or pub — all this gave him a feeling of having found a land free of all the restrictions and suggestions of oppression which he had come to accept as being there to offend him. Of course it is true that much of this was in his imagination; but since his painting had all to do with his imagination this fitted in too.

In the second phase of his artistic development, when he felt that to some extent he was unnecessarily dependent on the Western image, and he went abstract, a certain loss became apparent in the disappearance of this attachment to his Celtic sources. Soon, however, a new naivety set in with the adoption of found objects into his paintings. As these carried a certain suggestiveness from their former purpose, he took a roguish pleasure in finding new titles for the pictures which would give emphasis to the double meanings.

His final and most important period bound him up once again with his family origins and was consequent on the deaths of three of his brothers within a very short time. He invented an image for himself of a masked Pierrot so that he could, in a sense, be the main character in his paintings, showing himself mourning above the brother's grave or in one case entertaining the three brothers, all of them disguised as masked pierrots at the teaparty. During his last years he painted many highly romantic works with such masked Pierrot figures. These he usually placed in Connemara settings and he decorated the mountains and skies with a comb to bring out delicate, striated patterns suggestive of gentle breezes across the land and with clouds formed to indicate graceful figures floating in the heavens above.

These last dream-like paintings are of a type without parallel in Irish art records. They were received without surprise in the sixties when both in Europe and America an amazing eclecticism of style was commonplace and experiment was the everyday experience. There is, however, a quality of weightlessness in the figures, as if they were unaffected by gravity which introduces a new enchantment to the landscapes in which they are placed. The masked figures are quite impersonal and only emotions are invoked.

It might be argued that since Gerard was intent on pursuing an individual and detached role in his life generally, that he therefore wished to represent the visible world of the West purely as an observer and that he never felt the urge to place himself as a character in his own pictures until after his brother, Joe's death in 1962. From then on, he seemed to become a subject in his own paintings (perhaps the principal character). After the first tragic, mourning pictures, his work took on an idyllic atmosphere, almost as if he was hoping for a place of unworldly bliss ahead. Could these paintings have been in his anticipation of a kind of life which he had not previously considered and now felt deeply conscious about since he told his friends that he would not survive his fifty-fifth year?

During these last eight years, he had a number of illnesses and all his time was devoted to getting as much work as possible done whenever this was possible. Not only was he painting the happy Pierrot subjects but he was also deeply involved with the conquest of the printing technique in the Graphic Studio in Dublin, and most of his works here were based on paintings from his earlier life which he now cast into more tranquil variations, seen, no doubt, with the optimistic eye with which so many regard their youth.

I like to believe that coming towards the end of his life Gerard found an artistic means of expressing his deep longing for unity with the world of his dreams in Ireland's Western landscape and that his masked Pierrot symbolised his presence therein as that figure of comedy and gaiety which he so loved to impersonate in his various performances on the stage, in recordings still preserved on tapes and in his humorous anecdotes and conversations with his friends. Certainly it seems to be the fulfilment of those dreams of his boyhood years when nothing would satisfy him except to escape into the world of art as a painter.

LIST OF ILLUSTRATIONS

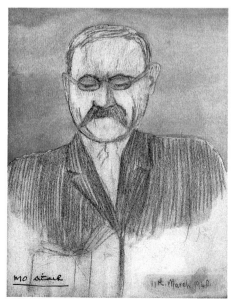

Above: Photograph of Gerard holding painting at an exhibition. Inscribed 'To Pino with love from Gerard'

Far left: My Father, drawing on 11 March 1940, pencil on paper, 7" x 5". From a sketch book

Left: My Mother, drawing on 20 March 1940, pencil on paper, 7" x 5". From a sketch book

1. Growing Up

There were eight children in the Dillon family, five sons and three daughters. The eldest, Patrick, was a most stable and reliable chap and following his mother's wishes he never drank alcohol. However, he followed his father's example in so far as he joined the British army during the 1939-45 war and he fought at Dunkirk. The fifth child, John, was also in this mould and as a young man he joined the regular British army and moved to England. Years later when they were living in London, if Gerard and his sister, Molly, saw John approaching in military uniform, they would dodge down a side street to avoid being seen talking to an Irishman in this uniform. Their inherited prejudices never left them.

The three children who followed Patrick in age, Vincent, Molly and Joe, were all striking individualists and quite opposed to Patrick and John in temperament. Their choices were always for music, dancing, drama, cinema and design. At that time the word 'artistic' would not have been used although they were certainly described locally as 'odd' because of their lack of conformity with those living around them. In due course Vincent went off to a seminary to prepare for the priesthood and subsequently was a missionary in the Argentine. Molly was a strong-minded girl with a real talent for dressmaking, handling materials and the like and was soon employed in the mills at clothmaking. When she moved to London she was highly regarded for her skill at turning out ladies' underwear and such like garments and eventually was in a position to buy her own house there. Joe was a singer with a fine voice but had never received any training in music. However he had a natural gift of voice production and with the family capacity to improvise was able to get occasional engagements in choirs. He soon moved into the fringe of musical circles, began to dress uncharacteristically for Lr Clonard Street and to be remarked on for his refined and somewhat effeminate manners.

The remaining three children were Anne, Teresa and Gerard. Anne, who was a twin with John, worked in the mills with Molly and subsequently moved to the USA where she married. Teresa was born delicate and died from TB when she was still a young girl. In those days that disease was rarely so called. Even in medical circles the term 'Consumption' was preferred but amongst the poorer classes 'Féar Gortha', the Irish for 'hungry grass', was used and people would say with pity 'she walks on hungry grass with the fairies'. In other words, 'she is not long for this world.'

Gerard, the artist, was the youngest. He was born on 20 April 1916. His sister Molly wrote to me from London before she died proposing to me that I should write this biography and gave a description of his earliest days:

At a few hours old, I took in my arms our new baby brother. His name in Mama's mind was never mentioned: but the other seven kids, four brothers not counting the new baby, and three sisters, we were all selecting names we would like for our new baby. Oh! the names we selected. 'Michael' after the archangel, 'Gabriel' also after an angel — was from two of the brothers, the eldest and the youngest (P.J. and John). These two brothers were not of our circle — they were tough. The youngest girl Teresa was five years old when this new baby came. Next day the 21st April 1916 — the week Ireland rose to shake the fetters held by the British Lion — Easter Week.

On hearing the names selected for our new, not pretty, baby — Francis Gerard, we were all very disappointed. Mother was a third order Franciscan. Hence the name Francis Gerard, the second one after the saint for expectant mothers (so we were told).

From the moment of his opening his eyes, I was in control, I being the oldest girl, then 8½ years old. The five others were younger. The only job with this new baby that I was not permitted to do was to bath him. All else was my job.

At six months old I was getting the shawl around my shoulders, to carry the baby. He waited for me to come in from school to take him outdoors. I never really heard or saw him laugh, always serious, a lonely child in appearance. His only way of expressing joy — he jumped and danced in my arms when in a warm shawl, where I always carried him. He never showed whether he loved or not — he was solemn and selective. I didn't realise this at the time, but I felt he was — well, just different: a good job. I wasn't tall at nine years old, as he was only about six months. One day I was hoisting him up in the shawl and he went right over my right shoulder and fell on his head. He never cried. Mama blessed herself and cried out 'Jesus Christ'. This I shall never forget and the fact that he never cried, endeared him more to me. So much so that when in school being taught about God and to love him, I felt that if the nun could see or hear my heart it would say 'I can't, God, I love our Gerard first'.

He was my life.

We were a group, the girls of our age, who had to nurse the younger members of our families. So we took these kids everywhere. When Gerard was able to walk, I walked the legs off of him. And we went far afield, Divis Mountain, Greencastle, the port near the sea, far away from the centre of Belfast: the outlet of the sewers lately, I have been told; to Bellview, far away from 26 Lower Clonard Street, Falls Road, near the big mills, more industrial than residential, small houses with large families. How our parents managed is a mystery to me now. No wonder on growing up, each one of us sought privacy, and did eventually seek to be alone. Our aloneness was self-imposed.

Gerard's second birthday gift: an unheard of thing with us grown-ups in those days. Our birthdays were never remembered. They were passed over and never encouraged by our parents. Gerard's was a large box of paints and a big book on which to paint (from Molly). At the time he only had his first gift, a sitting position dog, Jipp, which he loved and always kept near him. Until he died he was always terrified of dogs. His fear of them was pitiful due to his faith being shattered by our dog 'Tara' whom he fussed at and over-loved until one day she snapped at him and bit him around his nose.

Years later when staying in a cottage at Moyard, the nearest town was Clifden. He encountered a barking dog in a long lane. He turned and came back half a mile in order to get my assistance in handling the dog. I came back with Gerard. The dog met us barking. I talked to the dog 'Aren't you the nice one, your frock is all sticky with those old thistle tops. Come here till I take them off your dress'. Gerard walked past. The dog crawled on its belly while I took all the sticky things from its lovely black coat. Later I had to spell it out to him 'Don't show fear, just bark back at the dog.' But Gerard went his own way. His diary reveals this about dogs — not his fear, Oh No! but he said 'All dogs should be put down'.

During the Black and Tan war, our house was raided often — while our Papa was a night sorter in the GPO, we kids with our Mama were undergoing anything but a picnic. As a little boy Gerard showed great love for our Papa. He would go out on the stairs while Papa, who was on night duty, was trying to sleep, and he needed the sleep during the day. Gerard would bang with his hands on the bedroom door and sing and sing, then run down the stairs. This he kept up until Papa would really get cross, and he really did get cross, except in drink, and then Oh Boy!! awful. However he had promised Gerard to take him to the sea — he had so looked forward to it that he said to the other little children 'Who would like to be me?' to whoever said 'Me' he'd reply 'I'll bring you a crab'. He never did get to the sea, Bangor, with Papa. Although as a small kid he was at the sea. I took him with about seven or eight others of the same age. One of his works shows a scene — Donegal kids all playing and on a rock sits a small girl in a pensive mood wondering what it's all about; no one else on the sands only those kids and the girl herself. I was taller than the others and had to protect all of them. I wonder was that how he saw it?

On lampposts when girls and boys of my own age were swinging, I'd have Gerard with me. He would stand patiently and never complain and never run away. He'd just wait silently, blue with the cold. I'd get off the rope and open his little coat and put his little blue plump hands into his so small-looking pants-pockets. There he'd stand silent, patient while we enjoyed ourselves.

Looking back over the years we were like a flock of noisy seagulls, while the silent one looked on. Had Gerard been like most kids I would have been placed in a Reform school, but he never told on me, things I'd done — stole fruit from shops, even chased angry geese to steal their food. Once I was caught by the Cops — in the Falls Park; one large section was allocated for growing vegetables during the period after the 14-18 war. Us kids, after climbing Divis Mountain, on our way home, without fear or inhibition walked through this huge garden of vegetables uprooting turnips, carrots and the like and peeling them with our teeth. Evidently we had been watched and a Cop was in sight when we descended like gulls on the turnips and carrots. As no gates were open the city Cemetery was our only way of getting out. As the Cop came after us I had to cup my two hands for each one to give them a lift up on to the wall so that they could drop on to the other side. I was last and I couldn't make it before the Cop caught me. Most of them on the other side ran except Gerard and another small kid. My name and address was taken. The right name and the wrong address I gave.

Years later we were reminiscing and Mama said 'You were too young, even for the juvenile courts'. No wonder our Gerard disliked carrots and turnips afterwards.

Molly's whole life was dominated by her early experience in looking after and caring for Gerard. Like many young girls who are allowed to act maternally towards a younger brother, she came to regard herself as necessary to him. Until he was about six years of age and she had commenced to work, she cast herself in the role of his protector. This indulgence of the youngest child's wishes and pleasures is extremely commonplace in large families, especially when the older ones are out at school or at work. When they come home, the little fellow is unable to take part in the general ribaldry of family banter but is likely to be hugged and embraced by his sisters and at least given warm greetings by his older and more selfconscious brothers.

During these years too, Teresa was an invalid and she used to lie in a small bed beneath the kitchen-window looking out into Lower Clonard Street. The whole life of the family was lived in that kitchen and Teresa was thus able to participate in all the conversations which took place in the coming and goings of the family. From this time onwards, one of Gerard's functions was to fetch things for Teresa and to occupy her whilst her mother was busy. He soon developed a skill at amusing her with little pranks and he would dress up and make gestures and faces to amuse her.

Rosie Henry, who lived next door and would come in to play with them, can recall Gerard coming down the stairs in various costumes dressed up as a clown or an Arab and acting as he descended. Sometimes he put on a moustache or made up his face and he loved to take off the voices or the appearance of locals. Mrs Dillon enjoyed this as much as did Teresa and Rosie. As time passed Gerard continued this acting game until it became almost a part of him. Rosie believed that he had a real talent and always considered that he would be an actor eventually.

He never took part in the games played by the boys outside, neither football nor marbles seemed to interest him and he had no taste for the rough and tumble which involved most young lads. Soon he was mocked as an oddity for failing to participate in boyish activities but he seemed indifferent to this criticism. Occasionally he and Rosie performed a scene from Macbeth. Gerard had carefully learnt the lines and he was intent on finding a quiet place where he could stand and declaim the speech just like a real actor.

All his experiences at this time have left deep memories of a visual kind as he related in this anecdote amongst his papers which he called

Barefeet .... Belfast.

If it wasn't paddling in the Park dam you were, it was on the Park railings, with a jamjar catching bees. I called it the 'Dam Park' as small children will do, putting the cart before the horse. May was only in and the early spring just past. You couldn't get into your bare feet quick enough.

'Mother can I go in my bare feet now.'

'Ach Son, it's not warm enough yet, love.'

'I'm warm, honest Mother, go on let me in my bare feet, Mother, sure it's Summer now,' you plead.

'Oh I suppose I better let you. If I didn't you'd be just taking them off behind my back. But, here, mind you look out for broken glass in that oul dam and don't be coming back to me bloody and your feet in two, do you hear me? You're never near that oul dam but you come back soaking can you not keep yourself dry like a good wee fella. Now don't throw them socks just anywhere, you'll be looking for them before I will. Come back and put them shoes underneath the drawers, not lying in the middle of the kitchen.'

What relief, what freedom: to feel the hard pavers with the soles of your feet, and you can curl your toes over the edge of the crib and lift wee stones between them.

For a short while you find it unpleasant to walk over gritty ground but soon you can run across it with such ease that it might be velvet instead of a cinder track. All the new feelings you discover.

To walk across a shuck, a muddy patch at the bottom of a field, the sun has dried it, making a thin crust on top, your weight breaks it and your feet sink squelching into lovely mud. The feel of it oozing up between your toes to grip you coolly, tenderly around the ankles. The strange new plopp sound it makes when you pull your foot free. You have nice brown mud all over your feet if you're in the bog meadows and black if you're in the convent fields. Now you have mud boots. You let them dry until they crack and contract pulling your skin, it's a new feeling for you, it's lovely. When they start flaking off and you're tired of mud boots anyway, you go and look for a stream to wash them off.... imagine being able to wash your boots off ...what could be newer than that?

There is a lovely fast-moving stream, tumbling down from the mountain, from the hatchet field I am sure. You stand in it and let the swirling water melt the boots off of you. The fronts slowly disappear because you are standing facing the run of the water, so you turn your back on it, and then the heels are washed away. Two mud rings are left around your ankles because you weren't in deep enough. You look for a deeper pool near where there is a drop in the stream at the bottom of a gentle waterfall. By now your feet are too cold. Funny how streams are always in the shallows, covered in trees, keeping the sun out, as if the water wanted to keep cool.

You climb out into the sunshine and sit on a grassy hill. Now your feet are bare again, the only mud left is stuck between your toes and in your toe-nails. With a piece of grass and a stump of straw you finish the cleaning.

Playing in the meadow the long grass catches in your toes. Groping you get the stalk of a dog daisy between your big toe and the next one and with a sudden kick you rip the head of the daisy high into the air. The smell of a dog-daisy is like the smell of new corduroy trousers. Do old dogs wear corduroy trousers?

If you want to torture yourself you walk across a field of newly cut hay, your feet would never get used to the hellish prickly stubble. It often happens when a bigger boy wants to be cruel to a smaller one, he'll chase the barefooted boy over a field like that but he'll have his own boots on.

When it's summer and you're young, you thirst for new sensations, new feels. You look for a gap in a hedge with wire-netting. We called it netting wire. The nicest bit we found was around the tennis court in the Falls Park. You put one hand, palm flat, on one side, and the other on the other side. Then palm to palm you rub them together in a circular motion. Oh there's nothing as soft as this. They say it's like feeling a wee girl's bum. It's softer than moss on the feet, softer than half-melted tar on the sunny-side of the road, softer than new cow-clop. It's the softest thing yet, softer than anything I know, but it's not always easy to find a piece of wire netting where you can get a hand on each side of it.

When the day is over and it's bedtime, how much easier to wash your feet for bed. No shoes, no stockings to take off, and the dirt you get on bare feet is clean dirt. When summer passes and you have to be always in shoes and stockings you're always trying to get out of washing your feet. Your mother says 'Boy, you'll have to wash them feet of yours, wouldn't I feel awful if you were knocked down and taken to hospital with them dirty feet.'

Curse the ones who invented boots and shoes. They have taken all the 'feel' out of feet...

From a very early age Gerard was storing up memories like these of the feel of objects and surfaces, not to mention their appearance; and although he wrote these little anecdotes much later in life, because he had not the money to purchase materials for painting, the writing was fundamentally a substitute for expressing in pictures his nostalgia for mother, home and the thoughts of squelching mud and his childhood. 'Bare Feet, Belfast' is very much recalled in terms of the sensation of touch, but most of his other anecdotes are redolent of vision firmly recorded in the memory like, for instance this extract:

The rattle of the big red wheels of the country cart on the paving stones...rumbling along to the Friday market, eggs, butter and vegetables ... the Egg Man bent over his knees, sitting high up on the cart, hanging-limp hands holding the reins. Paddy-hat high on the back of his head, the brim down over his eyebrows, two purple-blue eyes staring out from a red-brown face.

Or this one about the Lamplighter:

The lamplighter on his rounds with the long pole that held magic, carrying it over his shoulder from lamp to lamp we would follow after him and as he struck the magic end through the little glass window at the top of the lamp we would gather round the bottom, our faces up-turned and arms out-stretched hoping to catch some of the magic as the light suddenly came on.

In general these recorded notes were avenues of escape from the daily encounters with having to live, as for instance 'The Brickfield Dam':

On the road leading to the kilns, steel tracks were laid, like shallow troughs, for cart wheels to run in, the horses walked between them where the ground was soft. The tracks were an inch deep and about six across and always filled with red brick dust, soft and beautiful like red flour. With both feet together we would shuffle along in these tracks making pink clouds fly after us. When we reach the end of the track we are no longer us, we are a tribe of wild red Indians and nothing on earth could be better than that. Who wants to be himself all the time?

These reconstructed memories of childhood always seem to imply the presence of other boys. Yet the only boy of his own age with whom he made friends in those early years was Joe McBrearty. They met in the Dunville Park, which was very close to the Dillon house and where Joe's father was the Park Ranger; and Joe lived in a house in the Park which probably seemed somewhat romantic to Gerard at the time. They were both about seven and began chatting whilst sailing boats at the fountain. Joe recalls Gerard's delight in being shown a bird's nest in a laurel bush just outside their house. Gerard refused to play other games but they made drawings side by side and Joe still recalls the strangeness of Gerard's pictures being commented on by grown-ups. From the beginning he tried to set down what he was imagining rather than what things looked like.

When he was about ten years old, Joe remembers that Gerard got a part in a chorus with a travelling company who were putting on 'Uncle Tom's Cabin' and he loved to sing a song which went

Poor Uncle Tom is gone away and we know that he's free,
Disturb him not but let him rest, way down in Tennessee.

Visits to the 'Silent' Films were also an important part of their growing up and Gerard has left a record of the battles he had with his mother to get out to 'follow up' films when he was bursting with the need to know what happened next. They used to go to 'the threepenny part' of the cinema which had forms with iron bars holding up the piece of wood that they rested their backs on. He goes on:

> The floor was stone and littered with orange peels and sweetie papers and there was an awful lot of ould 'dolls' with shawls who snuffed and asked you to read out the written bits of the picture (the subtitles) 'What she said to him' and 'What he said to her'. You tried to avoid these old ladies who couldn't read or hadn't their glasses with them. They'd no shame. They'd even call you from a few rows in front 'Here wee fella, come on up beside me and read it out for us.' .... And there'd be shouts of excitement at the frightening bits and calls of warning to the good fella when the villain was coming up quietly behind him 'Look behind you, hey! look out, Look behind you.'

Gerard left an impression of being generally aloof and the continuous involvement with the girls in Dillons' kitchen and the world of makebelieve he had developed for them marked him out in the eyes of the neighbours as precious, 'cissy' and superior. One woman described him as an 'ould Mary Anne', a favourite Irish term for boys of his kind. He attended the local Primary school in Raglan Street and later won a scholarship to the Harding Boys' school which was run by the Christian Brothers who were regarded at that time as very stern disciplinarians. This sternness and his continuing dislike of vigorous masculine activity resulted in him feeling very uneasy and wary whilst in the school. He was however highly intelligent and industrious and would never leave himself open to criticism or punishment if this could be at all avoided.

His older brother Vincent was away at the seminary whilst Patrick and Joe worked in the telephone section of the Post Office. Whenever possible Joe would be off with his musical friends and it was due to his contacts that Gerard had got into the chorus of the travelling 'Uncle Tom's Cabin'. Joe's conversation inspired Gerard with a desire to escape from the familiar round of local gossip and churchgoing. He longed to mix with those he heard about who were interested in music,

film, theatre and art. He could not quite understand how or why, but he felt instinctively that there was a life out there for him to discover. Anyhow he knew that the way the working people all around him lived was not what he wanted.

Joe McBrearty had gone off to join the air force and he subsequently became a priest and served as a senior Chaplain in the RAF during the forthcoming war. Gerard constantly besieged his parents to let him leave school and become a house painter and finally in 1930 at the age of 14 he was apprenticed to Sullivan and Sons, Painting and Decorating Contractors.

Saint Francis, oil on canvas, 29" x 18". Exhibited Five Irish Painters, Tooth's London 1951. Leicestershire Collection for Schools and Colleges. (See page 58)

2. The Early Days at Home

The Dillon family home in Lower Clonard Street, No 26, was just off the Falls Road in Belfast, now almost an enclosed Catholic area separated from other parts of Belfast by the agony of the conflict which has developed over many years out of the entrenched religious bigotry on both sides.

Only those who make contact with the families actually involved can realise the depths of this mutual bigotry. Mrs Dillon, Gerard's mother, was a classic example of this. When her family were growing up in the period following 1900 and the first world war, she carried in her mind a concept of Irish Nationalism which had hardly changed over a period of 150 years. In particular she regarded the Treaty which gave self-government to the twenty six counties and established the six Northern counties in 1922 as a total revocation of all she believed in. Indeed during the second half of her life anyone who sat for the Northern six-county parliament even under a Nationalist party ticket seemed to her to have moved over into the forbidden region of conformism with a kind of political compromise which she could not and never could accept.

She came of a family which had always held that Republicanism was the only political programme and way of life for those amongst whom she lived. They were Irish Catholics who had always resisted British rule and she could accept no alternative. Like their mother, those of her children who adopted this entrenched emotional viewpoint were to find themselves unable to understand their friends and associates who lived outside their local circle on this issue. And these friends and associates would soon come to accept in their minds that such Belfast people were unable to be reasonable and capable of seeing their point of view on any political matters which touched on the relationship of Northern Ireland and Britain.

The Roman Catholic Church in Northern Ireland stood for its people as the only certainty and security. Their priests understood their problems and situation and could distinguish between those who held strong Nationalist viewpoints and those others who had accepted the way of life which flowed from the current administration — employment, law and all the usual community services. Because of their priests' sympathy, the people tended to regard what was understanding as representing authority and, in time, the areas of separation got blunted. When groups of people were victimised or ill-treated, their pastors stood up and protested for them, and eventually the concepts of political nationalism and religion became almost identical in their eyes. And of course their need for comfort and support made them turn, particularly the women, to devotional exercises and involvement with religious ceremonies on a daily basis. Altars with lamps and flowers would be in almost every little Catholic house in the Falls Road area. Large coloured reproductions of the Sacred Heart and the Virgin were also commonplace and they were frequently seen as badges of political identity, necessary oppositions to the many images of William of Orange (King Billy) in the equivalent Protestant ghettoes.

Mothers like Mrs Dillon regarded it as their duty to instil religious practices and devotions into their families, not only by insisting on participation in church services but also by augmenting these with prayers in the home like the Rosary, the Angelus and frequent admonitions to the Lord, the Virgin and the Saints. Gerard has left an amusing record of his Mother calling her children to say the Rosary before they departed for their evening's social activities after their day's work.

It was about seven o'clock, the tea things were still on the table. John was in the scullery putting the last touches to his appearance, craning his neck in closely at the small mirror over the jaw-tub. Nelly was up the stairs changing into her best clothes; you could hear her high heels on the lino, she hummed as she dressed 't' was in a little Spanish town upon a night like this.' Paul had pushed back some of the delph to clear himself a part of the table and was quietly trying to do his homework. Other members of the family were about the kitchen, you could feel that soon the house would be deserted, only the mother and Paul left, she to do the dishes and Paul to go on with his 'exercise'.

'Here you John, you're not slipping out without the Rosary,' said the mother from a chair by the fire.

'Ach, Ma I'm in a hurry, I've to see my chum any moment now,' he grumbled from the scullery mirror.

'Yous are all the same. Yous wouldn't spare a minute to God if you could get away with it.'

'Couldn't we say it before bed-time, won't that be the same,' he answered as he came into the kitchen, looking spruce in his navy suit, the trouser creases sharp and clear, straight out from the 'presser' between the mattress and the tick.

'Oh I've heard that story before, yous are all good at putting it off. Oh yes, then in yous come one by one at different times, and some of yous sleepy and saying you'll not be able to get up in the morning till I'm sick of it and let you go off to bed, and bang goes the family Rosary for another night. I know yous of old.' Then she goes to the foot of the stairs 'Hey Nelly, come on down out of that and join the family Rosary.'

'Ach Ma, I'm late as it is,' moaned John.

'It'll only take a few minutes. You know what Our Lord says "If two or more are gathered together in my name ...." Paul come on and kneel down son.'

Nelly clumps down the stairs. The others begin to kneel.

'You'll make it quick Ma, won't you?' pleads John.

'If it was at the pictures yous were yous wouldn't want it cut short ... I'll be as quick as I can.'

She kneels on the hard tiles, her head high, her back straight. Some of the others grab themselves cushions and lean doubled over chairs.

'Here you Joe, kneel up straight, Oh yous must have your comfort, that's no way to face God, your shoulders all humped up, Mary get off your hunkers and kneel right, what a crowd.'

'I can pray better if I'm comfortable Ma.'

'I suppose none of yous can find your Rosary beads?'

'We'll use our fingers the night Ma, hurry up Ma' says John from the corner. 'You'll not do all the trimmings, sure you won't Ma?'

'I'll have to do some of them otherwise you'll not know what you're praying for.' Clearing her throat she starts 'INCLINE UNTO MINE AID OH GOD.' The answer came quick on the dot.

'OH LORD MAKE HASTE TO HELP US.'

They all circled around a picture of The Perpetual Succour, as they recited, she giving it out, they answering without hesitation, gabbling the Hail Marys at great speed with John in the lead. Soon they developed into a race. They were coming in with the 'HOLY MARY MOTHER OF GOD' before she'd finished with the first part. 'Ahem, Ahem' she cleared her throat. 'Will yous cut out that overlappin' it'll only keep yous longer in the long run if I've to be checking yous all the time.'

She offered up each decade as she came to them, for the repose of the souls of the Grannies and Granddas, for the health and strength of the uncles and aunts, jobs for the unemployed, peace and freedom for Ireland, the conversion of England and Russia. Before the fifth and last decade she'd offer it up for the safety of all peoples, that they'd all get back home, good and pure, safe and sound. If it happened to be a wild night she'd say 'Let us offer up this decade for the poor souls whose calling keeps them out all night in the elements,' then she'd pause and say 'Of course that includes the Peelers (policemen), but it can't be helped, they are somebody's rearing God help us .... OUR FATHER WHO ART IN HEAVEN.' At the end of the decade she'd go quickly into the long prayer beginning 'HAIL HOLY QUEEN, MOTHER OF MERCY, HAIL OUR LIFE, OUR SWEETNESS AND OUR HOPE, TO THEE WE CRY POOR BANISHED CHILDREN OF EVE ....' Resentful glances from John.

It's over and by the time she has struggled to her knees, some members of the family would be out and away. Paul would be back to his homework, and the mother would clear away the dishes into the scullery to wash, glad that once more she had achieved the family Rosary.

Those who still remember her, confess that she was extreme in these religious attitudes but nevertheless she was regarded locally as an organiser and a leader. During the month of May she would erect an altar in her house and neighbours would queue up in the street to come in, in their turn, to pray before it. If some of the young ones in the queue would make faces, others noticing would threaten 'I'll tell Mrs Dillon on you.'

She was firm and uncompromising but her good deeds are still remembered. One neighbour received a summons for slander which was probably false and she advanced the two guineas for the solicitor's fee for the defence and accompanied the neighbour to the court. Each Sunday when her collection for the African Missions was being made, a separate contribution of sixpence was made until the two guinea debt was repaid.

She was born Annie Foley and she married Joseph Henry Dillon after he had returned from the Boer War. This association with the British army was a matter of grave concern to her. In later life she could frequently be heard muttering 'There's the old fellow again, talking about the war'. Gerard made a clear record of one of those conversations, possibly at a time in London when he could not afford paint but felt, nevertheless, that he had to be creatively involved.

The mother and father talking about the troubles.

'God, if I'd my way with them boyos, I'd lock everyone of them up for a very long time, I'd have no mercy on any one of them.'

'Oh we all know that law-lovin' Johnny. Oh we all

know what they call you. Because you haven't the courage. A man that hasn't the courage to do what the're doing is no man at all,' replies the wife.

'Haugh, shoot people in the back, that's all they ever do, innocent people shot in the back, the dirty skunks,' he answers.

She screams at him.

'Is a peeler an innocent person. Innocent? Call them big over-stuffed murderin' brutes innocent, would you?'

'Ah for God's sake they're dealin' with mad fellows carrying guns doing more harm than good.'

'They're fighting for their country, God bless them,' she said piously.

'A fat lot they care about their country, the same fellows, they're just out for terrorism.'

'Terrorism be damned, that's just British propaganda, 'course it's just like you to swally everything they say, they're the greatest slurrers of people's good names, The British are past masters at throwing dirt. Sure we all know that.'

'Where would the country be without them?'

'Where would we be — We'd be free, that's where we'd be — free — and freedom is worth a lot.'

'Freedom to go hungry.'

'That's always your ould cry, always thinking of your belly, minding number one. I'm silly talking to you anyway, you're as British as themselves.'

'Who's British? I'm Irish and proud of it.'

'Irish, ha. The only thing Irish about you is the colour of your socks. You're like the Hibs. (The Hibernian Order) a flaming Green Unionist.'

'I'm no Hib. and you know that. I'm just trying to see the situation with a bit of common sense.'

'Oh, yes, always be sensible, you'll die of common sense one of these days. It's just that you hate seeing men with a bit of spunk.'

'Oh I like your brave men, getting women to carry their guns for them, they haven't the guts to carry them themselves.'

'What do you want them to do, carry them in their button holes, against the whole British army? Want them to go and give themselves up? Not bloody likely.'

'It's no use talking to you. You're a blind fool where Ireland is concerned.'

'Ah, go out if you're going out and stop dilly dallying with your Orangeman's hat in your hand — oul soldier — oul shite.'

Relations between them had steadily declined

over the years. He was well-built and strong and worked in the Post Office. He would leave home early in the morning and on his return in the evening would go to bed as soon as he had his dinner. Friends of the children can still recall his wife wickedly saying as he mounted the stairs 'There he is off to the Monkery', perhaps a reference to the development of a celibate life which had intervened over the years. He grew a beard and wore his hair very long for that period. His wife laughingly described this part of his appearance by gesturing with her hands against her shoulders and breast saying 'Hair to there and a baird to there.' The word 'beard' rhyming with 'hair' in her Belfast accent. A strong vein of humour ran through her character though her intense determined feelings were never far beneath the caustic wit she exercised so freely.

On one occasion a little girl neighbour was sitting with her outside the house in Lr Clonard Street, and their dog 'Barney' was playing around. 'I saw Joe Dillon coming down the road with his post-bag over his shoulder,' she relates 'and I said 'Barney Dillon, here's your Daddy coming.' Mrs Dillon took up the chant 'Barney Dillon there's your Dad...Barney Dillon there's your Dad.' Mr Dillon walked on past her through the doorway but she kept on derisively repeating it out loud. Then the door opened and he came out with a plate in his hand and threw the dinner she had prepared for him all around her in the street. But she went on laughing through it all.

Undoubtedly these conflicts between the parents worsened during the years, probably because Joe Dillon's drinking habits got worse. He became more and more silent and invariably went straight to bed after dinner. Yet Annie managed to communicate her humour and wit to the children and at least four of the eight were marked with a talent somewhat more than one might expect given their opportunities in life.

Annie Dillon's brother, John Foley, had a barber's shop and he was known for his talent as a musician. He had both a violin and a cello, which indicates the likelihood that the Foley family were inclined towards the imaginative world. He kept his cello under the stairs in Dillon's house and no doubt the occasional musical evenings took place there. One friend remembers that on occasions when there were no customers in the barber's shop, John Foley would take out his fiddle and play away to his heart's content. On another occasion in the barber's shop when John Foley was extremely busy the door was suddenly pushed open and a youth stuck his head in and said:

'Eh Mister, I'm short taken, can I use your lav'?'

John Foley looked him over with a measuring eye and replied

'Who shaved you this morning?'

'I shaved meself.'

'Then if you shave yourself shit yourself.' came the reply with devastating Belfast logic.

Annie herself could mimic cleverly and she would take off her friends in their comic moments. She also encouraged her children in whatever direction their imagination might lead them and dressing up and acting was part of their playtime. The interminable conflict between the neighbouring peoples and the continuing participation in their religious life meant that they lived in an atmosphere which was close to drama. Gerard's mind was stocked with the events and happenings of his childhood and many of these he set down as short stories or perhaps just painful excisions of memories of childhood. The following anecdote he called Wee Women Saints and Holy Souls:

My winters were filled with saints and holy souls. It was my mother was the cause of it. Any woman who did her duties and kept her dignity in spite of the hammerings her husband gave her, was a saint.

'That wee woman's a regular saint,' she would say about the woman who had just left the house.

'She'll get a big crown for it when she dies.' She was talking as much to herself as to us in the house.

'There's some people just made to suffer. Many's another woman wouldn't stick it, they'd just up and fly with a Kiltie, but she'll be rewarded, God is good.

It was difficult to imagine all these wee women as saints. I could not see them in crowns for some of them were ugly and wore shawls, and didn't comb their hair and snuffed and wouldn't suit crowns at all.

I thought and thought, how could you be sure you would become a saint when you died. The only thing was to grow up to be a woman, get yourself a bad husband, never neglect Mass, Confession and Holy Communion, and you have to have loads of children. That was according to my mother. But how could I grow up to be a woman? She never mentioned men-saints. Though there was always Saint Patrick who hated snakes, and Saint Francis who loved all animals. I was called after him. There was never any talk of him loving snakes or hating them. Yet he must have hated them for you couldn't have saints like that, one loving and one hating the self same thing, that couldn't be. Wasn't Heaven all harmony?

Though you could not see them the Holy Souls were everywhere. They made you know they were there, you could hear them plain enough on the wind, on any wild winter's night.

'What was that moaning in the chimney? Who was that whistling at the keyhole?'

'The Holy Souls of course. Ah yes, son, listen, listen. Do you hear the cries at the keyhole, and the moaning in the chimney? That's them.'

And you listen and there as sure as you're there, is the crying and the moaning. And your mother would go on telling you.

'Do you hear? That's them, Listen.' You sit silent and thrilled.

'You know we're not all made to do our punishment in Purgatory, some of us is sent back to suffer out our time on this earth. That's why you see the big deep doorways in the chapels and the thick hedges around the chapel grounds. Them's to give shelter from the winds and rain to the poor souls on a night like this.' In a hushed voice she goes on to tell you about All Souls night, when you leave a good fire on and the chairs set around it, and food on the table. That's the one night you don't redd (sic) away the table. You leave everything, and in the middle of the night the Poor Souls come in out of the night and have food and heat. That's their one night in the whole year.

Tingling with fascination, mystery and wonder, you ask her, whose souls are these now crying at the door and the chimney?

'Could be anybody's. Could be your Granny Foley's or your Uncle Rabbie's.'

When you are going to bed she would ask you to pray for their souls so that they might be freed and so enable them to get into Heaven. Their cries were to remind you, she said, that they were still enslaved in Purgatory, and she said, that may be only one, just one Our Father and Hail Mary was all that was needed to release them from their sufferings, and she would ask you like a good boy not to forget the Poor Souls, and she would say that when they get into Heaven, they'll start praying for you.

So you pray and the moaning stops, and you're sure your prayers have worked the trick, and Granny Foley has got into Heaven.

'Oh Mother the crying has stopped, does that mean my prayers have got them free.'

'Indeed they have Son. Listen, all's quiet now. That's the way it is. If you went down to Kate Dawe's you might hear the poor soul of her Bella crying at the keyhole. Then Kate would say a prayer, but it doesn't always work. Maybe you'd have to say a whole rosary before it would. Even then it might take more than that, the poor soul might have to do a few more years in Purgatory, you just have to keep on praying.'

Now my father wasn't one for talking about the Holy

Souls much. Though sometimes when you are scared of an examination in school, afraid you won't pass, he is apt to tell you to pray to the Holy Souls and ask them for help. And he would leave it at that. He would never go into details, but he would about Banshees. They are his weakness. His mother saw a Banshee once. He said he heard one once, but he said he'd be afraid to see one, for if you saw one you are sure to have someone belonging to you die. When his mother saw the one she saw, her aunt died in America, and that was awful, for she was going to take her out there. And if she had that would have made my father a Yankee and that would have made me one too.

My winters were full of poor souls, wee women saints, and my father's Banshees. It made the dark days and the wild nights full of mystery and other worlds wonders. It gave me a love for winter, and now when I hear the wild wind in the chimney, alas I have only the moaning in the chimney (what poor soul could whistle at a Yale lock.) I wonder is my Granny still at it after all these years. Was it possible that my prayers that night the moaning stopped released some other poor soul? My poor Grandmother's soul still crying away in the chimney, the moaning drowned at times by the playing radio. Poor, poor souls nowadays, they haven't peace to cry alone, always the late-night crooner to mingle his moans with theirs.

When the last midnight chime has faded away, the Holy Souls are left in peace, free to cry in the wind and moan in the chimney alone, all alone for the rest of the night long.

The Falls Road on a Saturday Night, oil on panel, 16" x 28", circa 1948. Douglas Gageby esq.
(See also page 81)

3. The House Painter

In later years, Gerard stated in an interview that he was brought up in Belfast to believe that to paint, which is what he always wanted to do, was not regarded as work in the family circle. 'So I was sent to serve my time as a house painter — that was not bad at all, for at least I learnt to be familiar with brushes and paint. But it became a bit boring having to cover large spaces with the one colour only, when my hand was itching to draw and compose,' he added. But it was noticed that whenever he could get a spare moment with an old piece of cardboard or discarded timber, he would make little designs and flourishes with the wide brush even though he was confined to the one colour.

He had probably forgotten that it was he, himself, who wanted to escape from school at any price. To be a house-painter was infinitely more attractive to him than almost any other occupation apart from finding his way into the theatre, to which he felt drawn all the time but for which he had no prospects and no opportunities. His older brother Joe who was working in the Telephone Co. had not been able to make his way into the musical world. Like Joe he had a good voice and his one experience on the stage, hearing the orchestra and seeing the cast, remained in his memory as comparable to a glimpse of paradise.

Each day at work he had to cope with washing walls and brushes, carrying pots and scaffolding for the tradesmen, boiling the pails of water and making tea. He also had to burn off old paint with a paraffin torch-lamp, remove old paper with a scraper called a shave-hook. For all this work he had firm strong hands and manipulative fingers even though when at home he could handle a needle and thread like the girls with whom he played as a little fellow.

He fell in quickly with the routine of the paint shop and was soon allowed to repair defective surfaces and to put on size and undercoat, to cut paper for the wallhangers and to paste it. Fellow workers of the time have said that his skill was soon apparent and before long he would look with contempt at the work of others which seemed to lack perfect finish. He would approach such surfaces and give them a flick with his thumb and forefinger and then turn away with a half concealed grimace.

All of this was an excellent practical preparation for one who could not bear art school. His mother once paid for him to go to night classes but he soon gave them up, as the idea of being taught what he felt he could himself do better merely left him frustrated. He continued to make sketches out in the garden shed in his spare time, for of course there was no place of privacy in the small house. Frequent visits to the cinema remained his greatest pleasure and he loved to go off alone to escape into a world of make-believe. However he did make some new acquaintances at work, with lads from different districts, so that he could set up relationships at his own level without fear of the jibes of Clonard Street about cissyness and stand-offish attitudes. He was determined and singleminded and never pretended to be a superior masculine type nor would he take advantage of those who were weaker or shyer than himself. He always stated his religious and political beliefs without reserve and he never pretended to crushes on girls in order to impress.

He admitted to those friends with whom he became intimate that he never felt drawn to girls. He told his best friend in the workshop that on one occasion when a Redemptorist priest questioned him on the subject in the Confession box he told the priest that girls did not attract him at all and said that his preference in this way was for men. The priest very unwisely told him that if he did not change this attitude that he would certainly be condemned to eternal damnation in the fires of hell. From this time on, Gerard avoided the ritual of the sacraments of Confession and Communion and gradually came to regard himself as a non-believer. To his logical and practical Northern mind, it seemed impossible for him to retain his faith in the Catholic Church any longer, although he kept up the outward show in his home because he could not bear to upset his mother. From that time onwards, the urge to escape from having to live this kind of hypocritical role took possession of him. The need for privacy, which Molly and Joe had already expressed, soon became his choice too. These three members of the family were ever after bound by an awareness of their individual characteristics and their dislike of having to relate to the doctrinaire rules of behaviour accepted in their home and locality.

They were motivated by the need for another kind of life where they could choose their attitudes, occupations and companions which would not be found wanting when held up to the light of authority as laid down in their mother's Third Order of St Francis.

The brothers managed to placate their mother when in the home, and their lukewarm attitude to religion she put down to their natural manly indifference. But in the case of Molly, open conflict soon emerged as she felt a deep responsibility to avoid allowing her to take risks. One night when Molly arrived home later than the expected late hour, she ordered her out of the house and locked the door behind her. Vincent, on holiday from the Seminary at the time, ran off down the road and having caught up with her, begged her to return when he would smooth over the problem. But she was adamant and would not be persuaded. She stayed away for a considerable period before a reconciliation could be achieved. She was working in a warehouse at the time and was in a position to support herself. It was about this time too that Joe decided to set out for London and try to make his way into the musical world of which he had heard so much from those of his friends who had already made the journey.

So Anne, who was also working in a warehouse, was the only member of the family left at home with Gerard and his mother and father. Patrick was married with a young family, John had gone away to the British army and Vincent was studying for the priesthood. Several years earlier Teresa had died, a death which was eventually regarded as a mercy so weak had she grown. The father and mother obviously felt that the reduced size of the family heightened the tensions that undermined their relationship. One day Gerard's nephew was despatched to the Clonard Picture House which his firm was repainting to bring Gerard home in order to settle a dispute between the parents.

They heard occasionally from Joe, now settled in London, and Gerard kept dropping hints to his mother that he would like to join his brother there. She was adamant however that he was too young but he half-persuaded her into promising that he could give it a trial when he reached his 18th birthday. She lived to regret this promise for the time came more quickly than she imagined and she found the parting from her youngest one of the hardest she ever had to bear.

He arrived in London in the early summer of 1934. He had never been out of Ireland before and the boat and train journey was a mixture of fears, uncertainties and excitements for him. When his train pulled into Euston, he felt a great sense of relief to find his brother, Joe, waiting in the crowd to greet him. Joe was a warm and kindly character, full of understanding for his brother's situation. He had arranged with the Saglietti family, with whom he was a guest, to let him bring Gerard to stay for a few days until he had found his feet.

The Sagliettis lived in Action Street in King's Cross. Mrs Saglietti had come to London from Italy when she was barely five years old, so the family spoke with characteristic London voices and had merged comfortably into the community. Of course they retained their loyalty to Italy and to Italian traditions, and the son, Pino, was a hairdresser by trade and a devoted opera fan. It was this love of opera which had brought about the friendship with Joe Dillon, who had a fine tenor voice but was not a trained musician as a result of which he was unable to get a start in the musical world. Pino and Joe had become very close friends and in fact in the Saglietti family Joe was always referred to by the name Brian. When he came to London, Joe decided that he would like to possess a more characteristically Irish name so he called himself Brian. Now Gerard had to mentally adjust to the fact that the Joe he had known all his life had suddenly become Brian.

Pino and Joe spent Gerard's first London days showing him the sights and their favourite haunts and they ended the first evening in the cinema, as much a favourite with them as with Gerard. From the moment of his arrival Gerard was attracted to Mrs Saglietti who was quick to respond to his lively, talkative ways. Soon she had him singing Irish songs and describing his life in Belfast and of course telling her all about his mother. Before long it was evident that Gerard found in her a most satisfactory substitute for the mother he had just parted from with such emotion.

After a short time, however, he and Joe moved out and found a room in the neighbourhood. There really never had been space for Gerard in the flat as it contained only two bedrooms. Furthermore Gerard, in spite of becoming so quickly attached to the Sagliettis, had come to London to discover a life of his own, one of which he had been dreaming about in which he would become a fulltime painter and would choose his own home, his own conditions, and his own friends. To all young

Above: *Forgive us our trespasses*, oil on canvas, 24"x18", signed. Exhibited Country Shop, Dublin 1942. PC

Left: *Dust to Dust*, oil on canvas, 20"x14". Exhibited Leicester Gallery London 1946. Noel Pearson Esq.

Overleaf: *High Cross Panel*, mixed media on panel, 44"x60", circa 1949. Exhibited retrospective Dublin and Belfast 1972/73. Private collection USA.

Page 28 top: *'Dun Aengus' The Aran Boat*, oil on board, 16"x19", signed. PC. (Dillon exhibited a painting *Aran Islanders in their Sunday Best* in the Victor Waddington Galleries in 1951 which could have been this picture.)

Page 28 bottom: *Medical Students*, oil on canvas, 18"x22", signed. Purchased by the Thomas Haverty Trust 1949. Ulster Museum, Belfast.

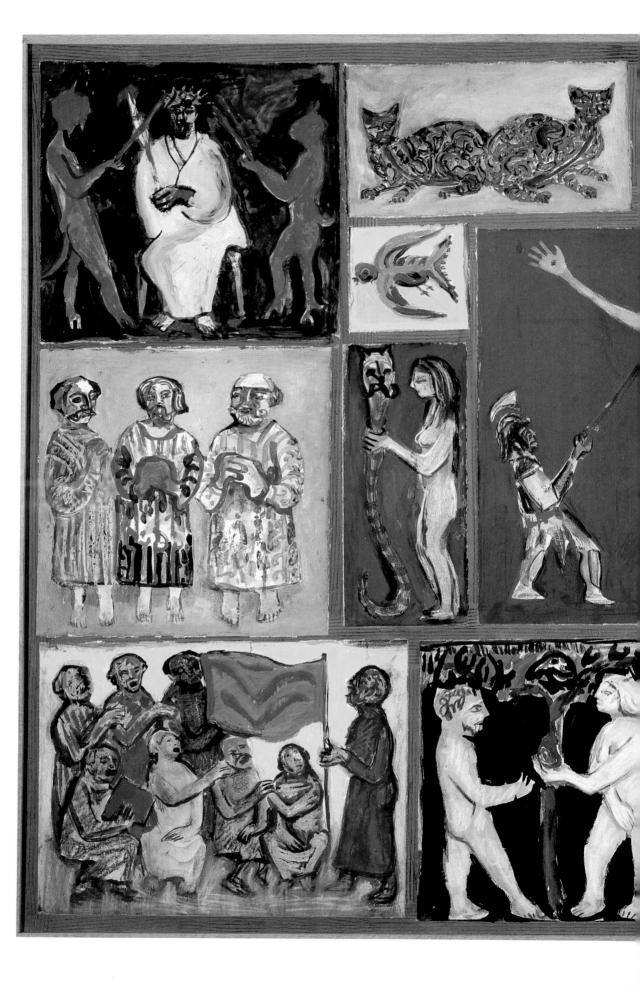

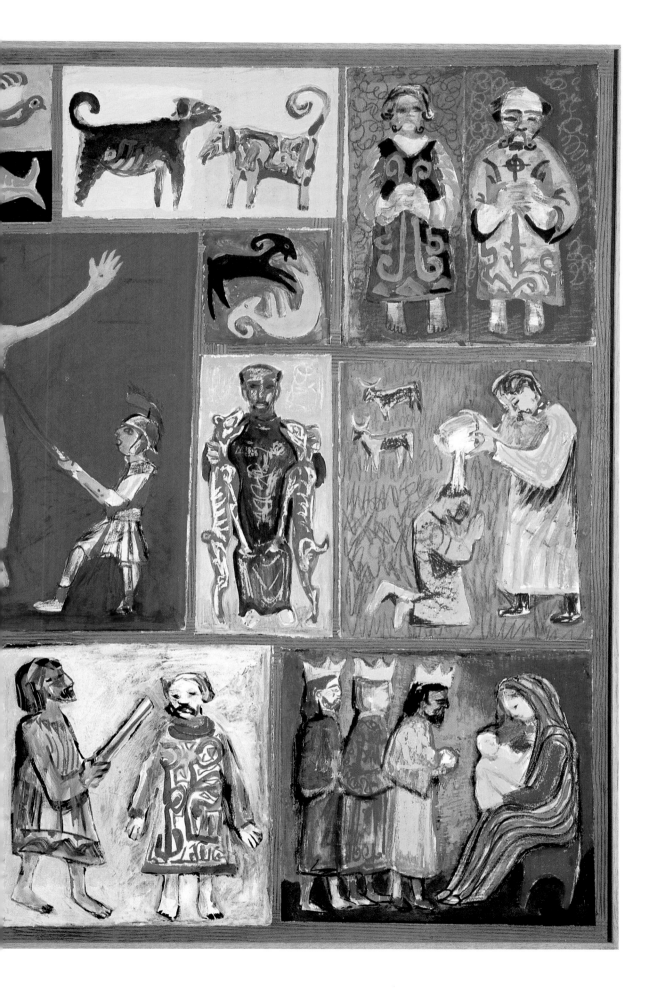

men of 18, starting life in a great city is exciting. To a young man leaving the religious bigotry and the narrow class struggles of Belfast behind him, London seemed a positive haven of freedom. Indeed London had long been regarded by Irish people of all parts as a place where the restrictions of race and religion, the narrow boundaries of behaviour laid down by church and family could be sidestepped or perhaps avoided altogether.

Gerard wanted quickly to find this freedom which beckoned. He had already found himself part-time jobs as assistant to house painters and he was able to keep himself in the frugal conditions to which he was well accustomed. Eventually he was employed by a firm of Decorating Contractors and was earning a weekly salary. This of course meant travelling a distance each morning and evening to and from his workplace and when eventually he got home at night he was weary. Sometimes he made sketches of things which caught his eye during the day and he made mental plans to get down to acquiring painting materials and moving to a room of his own where he would have space to spread himself out with brushes and tubes of paint. Very often he would call back to Sagliettis' for company and chat. Sometimes when he called Pino would be out and Mrs Saglietti would greet him warmly and give him a good meal. Then she would ask him to tell her his stories and when Pino had returned she would report to him:

'I fed him up. He doesn't eat enough I know. But we had a lovely time and he sang those Irish songs, the Spinning Wheel, and he told me stories.'

'Yes, but you can't understand his Irish accent properly,' Pino replied.

'Ah, yes, but they are so funny. He makes me roar with laughter.'

Pino had a collection of art books which Gerard enjoyed going through. He was always searching for clues on how to draw or describe certain positions or attitudes. Styles of painting or traditional old master techniques bored him because he had never acquired the trick of recognising from the paintings their period of production. He was unable to relate the figures or their background to the world they represented. European history meant nothing to him and virtually the only history he related to was Irish history as explained to him by his mother. If he saw a sculpture or a drawing he would interpret it in his own contemporary terms. If the figure represented was beautiful in his eyes he said so. That it showed Greek or Romanesque or Gothic attitudes to mankind caused him to twist his mouth in impatience. Every object or form was for him a shape to be abstracted and related to his own picture-making-mind, otherwise it did not count.

Nevertheless, Pino's interest in art of all kinds drew him constantly to the flat. In fact everything about Pino attracted him. That he was so close a friend of Joe no doubt caused him to feel jealous. But he soon overcame these feelings because he needed the affection of them both. They were both a little older and they acted protectively towards him. But Gerard harboured deeper feelings for Pino, which never received any open expression. Yet some years later in Belfast, when being questioned about his love affairs in London, Gerard confessed to his oldest friend 'I love Pino'.

Pino tried to influence him against the dangers of any indiscriminate behaviour in London. This came about because he had mentioned haunts which Pino knew to be unsavoury or dangerous. However Gerard had a ready ability to pull down a curtain of neutrality over his features, to change the subject and to move into new territories of discussion. Pino made no progress on the subject. Gerard had a private world of his own. As he began to learn about London he made friends with whom he went to clubs and cafes and whom he did not introduce to Pino's circle. He soon found that he had left a set of narrow conventions behind him in Belfast, but he also found new and even more confining conventions here in London. There were subjects you didn't mention, religion, Irish attitudes and politics. Anything to do with art or culture was regarded derisively by his fellow workers. So he tended more and more to consort with other Irish workers in London and to gradually cultivate the places where he would contact them. And he found the mysterious, anonymous, night life of the big city, something which was constantly attractive, because of the excitement which it generated.

But every so often he would be back in the flat with Pino and say 'Come round the galleries with me'. Then Pino would witness again this exclusive selection of works to which Gerard would respond because they contained some element of the kind of pictures which he would like to create. Everything else he dismissed out of hand. Years later when they were in Florence together, Pino took him to places like the Pitti Palace and was horrified when Gerard said 'I have no time for all that old rubbish, it has nothing to do with life and what we are interested in. I only like modern art.'

A valuable contact with home for Gerard at this time was Madge Connolly. She had come over from Belfast in 1930. She had previously known Joe when they both attended an Irish class there and a warm relationship had grown up between them. Indeed their families believed that there was an understanding between them, though this possibly never came to anything because of Joe's inability to secure himself a proper means of livelihood. Joe was a most attractive personality who tended to expect that the world would provide. Meanwhile he was in receipt of a dole. Previously on one of her holidays home she had called on the Dillon family and she found Gerard extremely anxious to learn about how he could get to London. But there was no way that Mrs Dillon would allow one so young to leave home. Indeed the mother's protectiveness to the family was all embracing. At the time she read all incoming letters and monitored all their activities.

It was with Joe and Gerard that Madge first met Pino and later when Molly Dillon finally made the break with home and came over to join her brothers in London, it was Madge who put her up. They seemed to settle into a quintet immediately, meeting almost every evening and visiting theatres, galleries and the like.

'We formed a little troop,' said Pino. 'Madge was called Val and Joe was called Brian. Molly, Gerard and I kept our own names. We were always together. This lasted I think till the war when we were forced to break up. We were a little coterie of young silly people.'

Four of these five young people had come away from home in search of privacy of movement and activity, yet they quickly reorganised themselves into a new and closed world of their own choosing, but this time away from parental supervision and the squinting windows of their neighbourhoods. Only Gerard maintained his own place of living and activity but now there was Molly to take her mother's place of admonishment, advice and concern.

Eventually the three Dillons decided to combine and to take a flat so that they could invite their mother over for a holiday. Their urge to get away from her dominating presence was hardly greater than their desire to re-experience it — the umbilical cord of their origins. Is there a clue here to the Dillon character and in particular to Gerard's? He would spend his life seeking to escape from his most strongly inherited instincts. Yet when he was finally equipped with the artistic means to express his thoughts and feelings, his subject matter would be closely related to his origins and upbringing. Religion, politics and his family background would be inextricably woven into the matter he was to set down in his pictures.

The Irish at Play, pen and ink on paper, 9½" x 7". Designed to illustrate *An Tóstal*, 1953, Official Souvenir Handbook. Published by Fógra Fáilte, Dublin

The Irish at Play

4. Early Years in London

It is hard to estimate how much painting Gerard actually accomplished in these first few years in London. Pino Saglietti recalls that he tried to persuade him to use watercolours more to give brightness and life to his drawings and to get working regularly. His own resistance to being taught — some stubborn conviction that he must find his way without help, certainly impeded him in his technical development. It is true that there is an advantage in preserving originality of vision but the actual handling of materials and the knowledge of preparing the ground on to which all kinds of paint have to be applied can only be satisfactorily acquired from the example and assistance of those already possessed of technique. All his early life Gerard was to feel a contempt for the tradition of the master-pupil relationship and in fact he had a horror of being seen to be influenced either by other artists or by fashions. Coming close to the end of his life he discovered the advantage of equipment, the techniques and the assistance of masters in the Graphic Studio in Dublin but one doubts if he ever reflected on his early folly in resisting all forms of help when he was first coming to terms with the technique of painting.

One suspects that when circumstances prevented him from making satisfactory images with his paper and pencil, he turned to his own kind of writing. Odd scraps of writings with richly described incidents have been preserved from these early days. Sometimes they have been re-written and polished up as several versions remain. One of these is dated 1937 and he entitled it 'Empty Room in London':

> When I was 19 or 20 I was in London for the first time away from home and feeling the freedom from home-ties, heady and beautiful. I was living alone in an empty room in an empty house in St John's Wood. Living illegally, I believe — as the owner didn't want to pay rates for an empty house and I believe rates have to be paid even if there is only one person living in the house. It was a four storied house and I lived on the third floor with only a bed and a cupboard, the bottom part of an old dresser that acted as everything for me, table, desk and food and clothes cupboard. For light I had a very beautiful brass oil lamp I'd bought for ten bob in the old Caledonian market up Pentonville Way. I had to live in the back room in case neighbours could see the light in the nights. It was strange and eerie. I had an old portable winding gramophone and one record — the father asking the son to come back to Provence from 'La Traviata' — this I played continually until the deep notes became nutty and rich to match the taste of beer and cheese-roll I'd taken to eating for my dinner. So that I can't ever hear that song without again tasting the new nutty flavour that cheese roll and beer was for me at that time. I came from a home where beer was an unknown drink — forbidden completely. I was very poor as this was the tailend of 'depression' but I was happy and beginning to paint a little and I frequented plays and ballets as much as I could. I read a lot and with friends went to pubs — a new experience for me. We were there to be somebody, to be one with a crowd — to look at people, to talk and laugh. So poor were we that one glass of beer in the night would be our lot. We sip this, making it last and carry the half-filled glass up our coats and go to the next pub up the street where the crowd might be different and so we spend many an evening. It was simple and we didn't demand more of life. I'm sure this solitary spell had a lasting effect on me all my life. I came to love living alone as I do still tho' I enjoy people coming to stay very much and I'm delighted they aren't with me for good.

> Being hard up I had to try and live as best I could as cheaply as I could. The woman I had the room from was at that time interested in buying and selling property so she had access to keys of empty houses 'to view' and she would kindly keep an eye out for me, such as the time she saw quite a lot of coal and coke in the cellar of one of these houses — I was loaned the keys and in the dark of night I would go back and forward with a sack stocking up fuel that kept me warm through the winter and all for just the labour of shovelling and carrying.

> It was on one of these trips around empty houses that I found lots of tubes of oil paint and hardened brushes all thrown into a basement cupboard. This was my introduction to painting in oils, once I started this I never stopped.

From his experience in the house-painting trade, he would have been able to cope with the old tubes of paint and the palette even though the major consideration of priming boards and other bases was something he took long to discover and indeed almost all his surviving pictures from this period must have ended up in the waste disposal bins.

His early subjects are casual reflections on the daily incidents of his London life and in particular of the ballets to which Pino had introduced him from his first days there. He had no sympathy for opera, which he saw in the same light as the old master paintings in the great galleries — symbols of the wealthy and powerful or intellectuals who failed to relate to the working class families from which he had come. The ballet, however, was frequently light, colourful and fantastic and seemed to find a response in his desire for movement and gesture and he delighted in making little sketches from Petrouschka and the like.

Probably the greatest attraction of London for him in those days was the night life to which he refers in the pen picture above. No doubt he found the daily round of work and return to the empty house a lonely existence and he finally brought it to an end late in 1936 when he decided to share a flat with his sister Molly in 56 Alexander Road, St John's Wood. There were frequent periods when no employment offered in the house painting trade. Early on, he and Joe worked as waiters in the Crystal Palace Hotel and later on he got night work cleaning shoes and acting as porter in a smaller hotel. During these periods when he could not allow himself to sleep he made notes of his experiences and sometimes turned them into short stories. One of these recounts the isolation and misery of a Christmas night away from home in London's West End and he uses the pseudonym of Peter to represent himself. It reads:

Oh Happy Christmas Night.

This Christmas was quiet for Peter. All attached people were busy in their homes with their children or parents or out enjoying themselves at parties, for after all Christmas was a get-together time if no other time was.

The streets were deserted as Peter walked his lonely way. The buses had left the roads since 4 o'clock this afternoon. 'Would there be trams running?' he wondered. The station was lit up alright, when he got there, but it seemed a strange place from the everyday one that he was used to, no bustling people this evening, no crowds of teenagers hanging about talking and laughing in stupid futility, with square tops to their tapering bodies, and womanish hair styles. Nothing now but the echo of some footsteps in the tunnel winding slowly down from the earth's surface till it reached the ticket box. After a long wait the train rumbled out of the tube into the lighted platform, and he boarded it and was on his way. When he reached the end of his journey he found he was too early so he decided to walk slowly through the back streets, looking into the sad shop windows — sad because they cried out 'Happy Christmas' from

cards wreathed and bedecked with holly and ivy, coloured lights and paper decorations. Cotton-wool-snow drifted clumsily down on threads to rest harmlessly on merchandise 'presents for Xmas' and now here was Christmas over at 10 p.m. Tomorrow would be St Stephen's Day better known in England as 'Boxing Day'. Some shops were empty. But in one, a painting was spotlighted in the centre of each window, no decorations here, no Christmas greetings, just one painting in each window. Wedding parties and happy gatherings of long ago. The men in crisp satin knee-breeches bowing politely to shy maidens with ringlets, in others bawdy-looking gentlemen forcing loving kisses on resisting ladies. In all of them tables loaded heavily with sumptuous food of all kinds. What a strange feeling these pictures gave Peter, these gay pictures in such lonely, sad windows in such grey, misty, deserted streets on a Christmas night.

There was no-one in the streets but himself, except a long sinister policeman he had passed by a few streets ago. Now he could only hear the heavy tread of this uniformed man and on looking back could see the blue white blink of his torch lighting up one doorway after another. Sad Christmas night. Peter thought about the paintings and wondered, did it ever pass through the artist's mind that his gay party piece would one lone Christmas night be sadly illuminated in a back street window in St James', to be looked at by a thoughtful young man on his way to do a night's work. The merry paintings only made Peter more conscious of being alone in these deserted streets. They made his mind wander off from the silk and satin clad marionettes on canvas to his childhood, to Christmases in the past when he wasn't alone. Then a feeling of fear took hold of him. A feeling of being alone in these grey, misty, badly lighted streets, with nothing but a sombre policeman somewhere about, dressed up effigies and the sad-gay pictures by obscure artists. That he had no right to be alone in these streets, alone near these shops, a loiterer, an object of suspicion. So he walked quickly on so that if observed by any pair of unseen eyes he'd appear to be going somewhere. Then out of the quietness came the sound of feet, more than one pair. He walked more quickly now, but pricked up his ears for any sound that would give a clue to what and who it might be. From the corner of a narrow lane, three figures came, two large ones half pushing, half carrying the smaller form of a young fairhaired man, about 26 years of age. As they quickly came and passed Peter he looked almost without seeing. The expression of hopeless-ness on the captive's face stayed long in his mind. The two large figures were of a policeman in uniform and the other in plain clothes, each had a vice-like grip on the young man's arms bent up his back. That expression, what did it remind him of? Peter found it hard to put words on it. That awful look, the silences of the whole happening, nothing but the movement of feet hurrying determinedly onwards, Oh Happy Christmas Night. It was only when he reached the brightly lighted front door of his place of work that Peter could put words on that face. 'Like the face of a drowning girl,' he thought.

It is always memories charged with his visual imagination that mark such little descriptions as these. Gerard had the capacity to find compelling incidents with which to complete his story but he must nevertheless have been impatient with himself that he had not the resources to turn them into paintings in which his romantic mind could find the outlet for the expression of his characters and the atmosphere with which they were surrounded. Not many of his paintings prior to 1939 exist. He worked on an experimental basis and destroyed three out of four because of their technical failings, which he could recognise but could not correct once they had been completed. Most of those which he kept were later destroyed by bombing in the premises run by Madge Connolly and Pino Saglietti in 1943. They had kindly taken them in for him and they were unfortunately wiped out with everything else at the time. The occasional picture which had been sold or given away depends very largely on figures or objects marked with qualities which evoked past memories or in some other way enabled him to build up a series of images like a poem, to recreate the nostalgia of the place from which he had escaped but which he longed to re-experience.

The process of finding pleasure in his blending of colours and forms to subtly suggest time, weather or other mood effects was never to be a strong element in his work, until the time came that with experience he felt totally in control of his materials.

Once he moved into Molly's flat, he was immediately exposed to her maternal concern to see him fulfil his destiny as a painter and she constantly chided him if she felt he was neglecting to apply himself to his painting. Above all she admonished him not to be wasting time 'galivanting around pubs with wasters when God gave you such a talent'. Her belief in him was profound but her fears for his lack of application were such that she was a source of irritation to him and he began to conceal his pictures from her because he was hurt by her caustic tongue and did not believe that she was a competent judge. Her sharp Belfast chidings, however well meant, seemed to him as insults to his latest creations.

One of his close friends was a New Zealander, Ernie Atkins, also interested in being a painter. He was a keen outdoor man and involved Gerard in cycling, rowing and in general getting away from London into the remoter parts of the countryside. Finally they planned a cycling tour of Ireland and having organised themselves with tents and the necessary camping equipment they travelled over in the summer of 1939. Apart from short journeys into the mountains around Belfast when he was a boy, this was Gerard's first experience of the Irish countryside.

Molly had brought Gerard to Dublin for the annual Easter Parade in 1928, twelve years after his birth and the Easter Rebellion of 1916, because she wanted to stimulate him with nationalistic ideas and because she had a romantic belief that eventually both Northern and Southern Ireland would be united as a Republic. She saw him, perhaps, as the future painter of the united Ireland which was the basis of the hopes and beliefs of all the Roman Catholics of their class in Northern Ireland. As a result Gerard's image of Ireland was limited to his Belfast environment and his one-day trip to Dublin. He must have seen it imaginatively as a sort of political conception with the idyllic overtones that relate to the purely imaginative.

Cycling around the Irish countryside with Ernie Atkins, he was forced to face a totally new concept. The life of the simple farming people or of those living in towns or villages differed little from anything he previously knew, but he was surprised by the changes of costumes, speaking voices and general easy pace of the life of the people. Those living in the Midlands differed least in their life styles from what he was accustomed to in Northern Ireland, but his first glimpses of Connemara with its mountain ranges and rugged coast-line took his breath away. Many of the people spoke Irish and even when they spoke English, they made it sound like a different language. Something of its freshness and the simplicity of the lives lived by the people caught him unawares. For the rest of his life he was to be moved to see its surroundings and its occupants as the visible symbols of the country he had dimly dreamt of and idyllically desired to belong to.

He had, of course, seen the paintings of Paul Henry and John Keating of Achill and Connemara and in fact these had become commonplace in England where they were used as posters in Railway Stations, but he had somehow come to regard them as costume pieces, partly invented by the artists. The discovery of this landscape broken up by stone walls and punctuated by huge boulders of limestone, too large to be removed from the fields, provided the white washed cottages and the animal life with a background which fascinated him by its patterns and painterliness and delighted him because he felt that it was he who had discovered it. Many years were to pass before he could cope with its broad effects, but its immediate effect was to give him a new ideal in terms of subject matter.

Then suddenly all was disrupted. War was declared and they had to collect their possessions and make for the coast to return to London. To his dismay Gerard was refused permission to embark, as he had no intention of joining the British Army, but Ernie Atkins immediately announced his intention of joining up and he left without his friend. Fortunately Gerard's possessions in London were in Molly's flat and he returned to join his family in Belfast. Here he was to experience, with extreme bitterness, all the confining effects of living on the edge of the Falls Road and belonging to a group of people who were extremely unsympathetic to the British war effort and supportive of Southern Ireland's neutrality. The situation in Belfast was now aggravated by the regulations about Black-outs, ARP and rationing. The family had to queue up for ration books and a new dimension of supervision by Police and Army was introduced. It became impossible to ignore the conditions imposed by war and to adopt the previous attitudes of ignoring as far as possible all signs of political authority.

Two of Gerard's brothers were in the forces, Paddy and John, both married and with families. Molly had returned from London for a short time but found conditions unendurable and succeeded in getting back by declaring that she was going to join up. However she was skilful enough to avoid this and obtained satisfactory employment in the ladies' underwear business in which she was already skilled and in fact remained successful there all her life. So the Dillon household in Belfast in the first year of the war consisted of Father and Mother, Joe, Anne and Gerard.

From the moment of arriving home, Gerard found Belfast a most unwelcoming place. There was tension in the family caused by his father's sympathy with the British war effort in contrast to his mother, who, in spite of her concern for her two sons in the forces, felt that she was enduring an impossible situation. Deep down

she rejected any idea of members of her family being involved in a war on the side of Britain, which all of her life she had regarded as enemy and invader of her own territory and national surroundings. Furthermore the Irish Free State, as it was then known, the 26 counties of Ireland now separated by a border, was preserving its neutral position and had a German Ambassador and staff in residence in Dublin.

Naturally Joe and Gerard shared their mother's feelings but outside the home they found themselves pushed into a position where their normal expressions of their Nationalist sympathies were less well received than formerly, since so many people were now involved through relations and friends with members of the forces or were part of the security services, First Aid, ARP and the like.

One of the little stories which Gerard wrote at this period he entitled 'The British Army as The Falls Road Contraceptive' and this may well have been inspired by his mother's bitter reflections about men who changed their political allegiance during the conflict at the time. It reads:

Eamonn married Nelly during the depression, she was only seventeen and he just turned nineteen, they hadn't a hope of getting a place of their own, but they considered themselves lucky as Nelly had lived alone with her widowed mother. She was long, tall, sour and old and unlike her daughter had married late in life and so they could live with her. Eamonn won the old lady over, it was seventeen years since a man had lived in the house. She gave him great scope, he tore out the old dusty shelves which lined the kitchen, made the bad walls good, replaced the oldfashioned wallpaper with the latest, shared his Zane Greys with her and all went well. Every year or nearly every year a child was added to the household, for Nelly was mad about Eamonn. By the time the war came they had seven of a family. The old mother-in-law's bones started to show more, her mouth soured more, she was getting old and tired, and started looking on Eamonn with a disapproving eye, as if it was his fault.

'There's enough childer in this house now, these old houses were never meant to house so many.'

'Are you fed up Mrs McGonigle, are the kids annoying you?' Eamonn replied. He still called her Mrs McGonigle after all these years. She had melted towards him when he first came, but she was the kind of old lady who couldn't melt beyond a certain point, so Eamonn never got around to calling her Maggie.

He and Nelly talked.

'God, girl your ma seems to have called a halt to the family.'

'Take no notice of her, boy, she doesn't always mean

what she says.'

'Still an' all it isn't very easy on a fella if he's always gettin' digs about the size of the house and the size of his family.'

'You're too sensitive boy, she's just tired, ever since she got retired out of her job she's always in the house with more time to think; God it was much easier for everybody when she went to work every day.'

For all Nelly's talk, Eamonn didn't feel easy in his mind, the war against Hitler was at its height, and Eamonn and a pal of his joined the British army. When Nelly heard the news, she cried bitterly, she loved him so much and now she was going to be without him for such a long time, this was an awful war, it might last for years, and Oh God, there was the danger that he might never come back, they said this was the worst war yet.

'He did right' said old Mrs McGonigle 'if I was a young fella I'd do the same meself' but Nelly cried on.

'Now we'll have room to spread ourselves out, Rosaleen and Gemma can sleep with you and that will give me more room' said her old mother.

'Oh, ma you're very selfish, what did you go and be always hinting like that for, you know what he's like, you'd think you'd have more sense. God if anything happens to him you'll have an awful lot to answer for.'

'Now, don't be a silly girl, you know bloody well that he's only pleasing himself. Nobody could drive Eamonn where he didn't want to go, and well you know how mad he's always been playing at soldiers, the way he kept that old bandolier polished up. For what? I ask you. Sure wasn't he in the I.R.A. when you met him and wouldn't he still be in it, if you hadn't made his life a hell, wouldn't he still be in it, sure you know that. Tryin' to make out it's my fault.'

Eamonn preened himself in his brand new khaki uniform.

'Girl, I've to go across the water tonight' he says putting his hands on Nelly's shoulders, she bursts into a fit of sobbing and he draws her to him. She cries hard as he holds her tightly in his arms, his own eyes fill with tears, and overflow down his cheeks.

That night he sailed away into the black-out, into the war, and Eamonn and Nelly's family stayed at seven for some years to come and old Mrs McGonigle was very pleased.

Gerard's mother was not only bitter emotionally. She was also strong-minded and aggressive and on one occasion she let her feelings get the better of her. He later wrote the incident as an anecdote, changing his mother's appearance but otherwise recounting it as he had witnessed it and as many others had heard it. He called it 'Young English Soldier':

Down at the bottom of a long dark passage was a square scullery with a door and window opening on to a tiled yard. The scullery had the usual sink or jaw-tub, a gas cooker and in one corner a big bulky gnarled-looking mangle. All around the walls high up, ran a broad wooden shelf. This scullery wasn't the brightest of places. The troubles were at their height. Three or four soldiers were in raiding the house, two did the upstairs and two the downstairs. A green young soldier was in the scullery. He'd searched in the dark hole behind the stove, the space under the sink, the dirty clothes box, the bundle of clean ones sitting on the mangle ledge, the low shelves — no guns anywhere, no bullets even, not a bomb in a bowl or mug. 'What's on top of the shelf, Mam? Any rifles, any arms of any kind?'

'You're doing the raiding, son, it's up to you to have a look,' said the lean, grey old woman.

'How do I get up?'

'Just whatever way you like, son, you can climb on the mangle,' she said.

'Here, will you hold this, Mam', he gave the old lady his well-polished rifle, with its bayonet fixed on top, and climbed on to the mangle, and was craning his neck to have a look along the shelf. His thick puttied calfs were near the old woman's arm. She stepped back, raised the rifle to her shoulder professionally, tapped his buttock with the point of the bayonet blade and said 'Here, what would you do if I blew the arse off you?'

He jumped down with mouth and eyes wide, took the rifle from her and stumped out into the yard to continue his search for arms in the watercloset and coal shed.

Belfast itself was less inviting during the blackouts which caused a slowing-down of night life and a reduction in entertainments of all sorts. The local pubs around the Falls Road seemed to Gerard greatly dissimilar from those he was used to frequenting in London, and as far as art was concerned, nothing seemed to be happening.

Eventually he decided to move down to Dublin to see if he could find something like the freedom he had previously enjoyed in London.

Above: Drawing of Gerard by Daniel O'Neill, pencil on paper, 5" x 6½". Inscribed verso 'Myself sketched by Dan O'Neill 1944'
Below: The Dreamer, oil on canvas, 16" x 20", signed. Exhibited IELA, 1956. Dunadry Hotel Belfast. (See also page 76)

5. Dublin in Wartime

The coming of the second world war had a surprisingly beneficial spin-off for the artistic life of Dublin. The restrictions in travel both in and out of Ireland forced organisers in various disciplines to rely on native artists. This applied particularly in the case of theatre. Travelling stage companies in most cases ceased to be available and the two principal repertory companies in Dublin, The Abbey and The Gate, quickly grasped the opportunity to experiment and to extend their range in order to capture the floating audiences no longer provided for by the big names from London and New York, who normally played the revue houses.

In the case of the visual arts, there had already been a breakthrough in public taste for those working in the cubist and expressionist styles and The Victor Waddington Galleries (ultimately to move to London) catered for such collectors. In October 1939 a new organisation was opened called the Contemporary Picture Galleries in 5 South Leinster St. with a Loan and Cross-Section exhibition, featuring Braque, Picasso, Gleizes, Gris and Dufy and various modern English and Irish painters. They moved the following year to 133 Lower Baggot St., and in November put on an exhibition of six Irish painters who had studied at L'Academie L'Hote in Paris, Evie Hone, Mainie Jellett, Norah McGuinness, Jack P. Hanlon, Eugene Judge and Harriet Kirkwood.

Slowly too, an influx of artists from abroad began to assemble, presumably to enjoy the almost peace-time conditions in Dublin as well as to avoid the danger of conscription in their native countries, and they took premises in Baggot St. where they held exhibitions and lectures. They called themselves the White Stag Group and they invited into their ranks adventurous young Irish artists and gradually began to gain notoriety. They invited the most distinguished English art historian of the day, Sir Herbert Read, to come to Dublin and to write an introduction to one of their catalogues. In this he declared 'Wars don't interrupt the course of art. Here in Ireland, not only has art found a secure shelter but even a fresh vigour.'

There was an atmosphere of adventurousness in the air at the time, possibly a reaction from being shut off from the rest of the world by the wartime conditions and undoubtedly also by a desire not to be seen to vegetate in the somewhat privileged climate of neutrality. On the 12th January 1940, the students in The National College of Art invited Mainie Jellett to lecture to them, aware of her experience after a ten-year apprenticeship with Albert Gleizes in Paris which she and her fellow artist, Evie Hone, undertook from 1921 to 1931, when all three set out to explore the basis of Cubism and in Gleize's words to follow 'a long, prudent, methodical, undertaking leading to an end intuitively foreseen, movement and integral object.' In fact their quest was mainly to justify the making of a painting as a composition with forms and colours created without any dependence on a subject in anatomy or nature or indeed on any shape already part of the repertoire of normally recognised images. At the time the teaching in The National College of Art tended to follow the time honoured academic principles upheld by The Royal Hibernian Academy, from whose ranks many of the Professors in that College came. The students' call to Mainie Jellett was therefore something of a cry for change.

Other artistic bodies also sought stimulation from outside and The Friends of The National Collections, whose function was to acquire works for museums, invited distinguished authorities, including Sir Kenneth Clark, then Director of The London National Gallery, to lecture and they acquired various works of modern art such as Rouault's 'Christ and The Soldier' and later a fine bronze by Henry Moore. Both of these works were offered to the Modern Gallery in Dublin but were refused, largely because the committee responsible were out of touch with contemporary art standards. Immediately the Rouault was rejected there was a public outcry because it was felt that this work was not only excellent but also an example of religious art close to the sympathies of the Christian population of various creeds. The outcome was highly beneficial to popular art appreciation. The general public were aroused and supported protest meetings chaired by Church dignitaries. The outcome was that the major Catholic seminary in Ireland, Maynooth College, accepted the Rouault painting on a temporary basis until such time as a more broadminded committee took over the modern gallery.

This was a time when the arts came to occupy a new importance in the life of the community and no doubt the resulting publicity attracted the interest of Gerard. When he arrived in Dublin, he took a room in Blessington Street and then set about finding some niche in the art world which would enable him to make contact with other young painters and the kind of people with whom he longed to associate. However he knew none at first and in a letter to his friend, Madge Connolly, in London, he recounted his intense loneliness and told her that he was sitting on a bench in St Stephens Green Park and wondering if he might chance opening a conversation with a lad nearby. A passer-by hailed this lad 'Hello Gerard' and he took the hint and said to him 'That's funny, my name is Gerard too'. Then they got talking and it transpired that they also shared the same surname, Dillon. He attended the exhibitions which regularly took place in The Dublin Painters Gallery and eventually introduced himself to Mainie Jellett, the highly regarded leader of the modern art movement in Dublin. For many years she held classes for students in her studio in the family home in Fitzwilliam Square and was a superb teacher. Having had such opportunities herself, first with Sickert in London and later in Paris with L'Hote and Gleizes, she experienced the missionary's desire to pass on her understanding of the basic nature of design and composition which she felt was a necessary adjunct to the technique transmitted to pupils in academic circles, particularly in places where the conflict between modernism and academicism survived. Her teaching was directed towards transmitting an understanding of form rather than of following the more limited approach of representing nature by the process of shadowing in greys, which one of her group described as 'slow photography'.

She commenced by arranging a still life from a range of objects which she kept nearby — a top hat, a bottle, a vase, a violin and three architectural columns as well as a complete model of a classical building. She insisted that the student should learn to construct the curves, content and plastic nature of the objects, however ineffectually, in order to realise their sculptural dimension rather than just the outline. This was an extremely difficult and frustrating method which soon weeded out the weaker ones and resulted, in fact, in turning the present writer from painting to art criticism. But for those who stayed on to assimilate the method, it was responsible for a new and exciting generation of young Irish artists, ultimately resulting in the creation of The Irish Exhibition of Living Art opened to the public for the first time in September 1943, with Mainie as its first President.

Luckily for Gerard, Mainie recognised his possibilities. She instantly responded to his sincerity and intensity and his uncompromising manner of expressing his distaste for photographic representation. Accordingly she encouraged him to put on an exhibition of his paintings in the Country Shop in St Stephens Green, one of the best venues on a busy thoroughfare and beside the fashionable hotels.

The exhibition was opened by Mainie Jellett on Monday 23rd February 1942. She began by pointing out what courage a young man required 'to launch out on a painting career at a time like this, with the forces of destruction rampant, whilst the forces of construction were struggling for life'. She stated that it was especially necessary for the public and the artist to realise their combined responsibility, one for the other. 'Art is not escape' she said. 'It is a force that can inspire and strengthen and at the same time soothe, but for this to happen, the artist must give of his best and be absolutely sincere — otherwise he is betraying his vocation. The public, too, have their responsibility towards the artist, particularly the young artist who is genuine, not just clamouring for notoriety at the expense of all else. The public' she reminded her listeners 'must have an open mind and be ready to receive the emotion and ideas generated by the artist and this produces the necessary ebb and flow of ideas and emotions which nourished the artistic experience and produces the living contact between the artist and his public.'

These were noble sentiments to warm the heart of a young man who had not previously succeeded in breaking into the rather anonymous arena where he could feel himself to be a practising painter. The press received the exhibition warmly at a time when art criticism was more spasmodic than regular. Photographs showed Mainie Jellett and Gerard (page 40) looking at 'Petrouschka' which she had warmly praised in her opening speech with to its left 'Winter Sunlight' of which the *Irish Times* art critic on 24 February wrote 'The Dublin Quays turn to radiant poetry'. Some of the pictures included were reflective of the terrible war damage Belfast had suffered in previous years' air raids, 'Result of a Raid', 'Bombed Street' or 'Blitzed Landscape'.

Above: Photo of Gerard with Mainie Jellett at the opening of his first one-man show
in the Country Shop, St Stephen's Green, Dublin, 23 February 1942
Below: Dan and Gerard at Contemporary Picture Galleries, Dublin, at the opening of their exhibition there in 1943

Another picture of war conditions was called 'Shades'; 'a study of a sentry standing outside his box, he manages with a few white lines that are quite in harmony with the scheme to suggest the pitifulness of the subject' said the *Irish Times* art critic and he also mentioned the fact that 'the artist was set musing by a visit to a church and the sight of the people going to Confession and praying before and after confession, and the result is the touching little picture 'Forgive Us Our Trespasses' (page 25).

All of his pictures produced at this time reflect his gift of reportage, combined with his eye for significant shapes, both of people and places, and in 'Bombed Street' he seemed to give almost equal value to the inhabitants carrying away their bags and to the wrecked houses, both described with thick impasto and broad brush strokes.

When Gerard arrived back in Blessington Street on the night of his first exhibition, a telegram awaited him announcing the death of his mother and calling him home. His mother was central to his life and all his prejudices and foibles were interwoven into the experience of growing up as her baby and youngest son. His writings reflect how well he understood all this but nevertheless the sudden shock of her death on the day when she could have shared his first success was a blow he could hardly absorb. He was unable to express his grief as others can, but he adopted a serious withheld poise, as a result of which he allowed the pain of the separation to enter his soul and linger on indefinitely. The fact that his mother and father had an uneasy relationship for many years had encouraged her to turn to her youngest child for affection, a fact probably arising from his deep sensitivity and instinctive awareness of her private feelings.

Fortunately Gerard had the excitement of his first ever one-man show in the Country Shop in Dublin to draw him away from Belfast and those painful times in Lower Clonard Street where the memory of a lifetime's affections was suddenly removed and replaced by the sullen shadow of his father who was also suffering but unable to surmount the barriers which had grown up over the years, and who now tended to live in a solitary and withdrawn manner.

Gerard was able to travel frequently between the two cities. The train service was good and reasonable and the journey took less than three hours. Dublin now began to open to him and he made friends with other artists. In particular Mainie Jellett was kind and

sympathetic to him in his grief; though he was unable to take lessons from her she no doubt saw that he had an instinctive quality of setting down images with a fresh and personal touch, almost reminiscent of a conscious primitive like Christopher Wood, the then very popular painter in Cornwall. She invited him to use her studio to paint in. There he could see the set-up for her students in the fine house in Fitzwilliam Square, where incidentally there was a constant presence of music. Mainie herself was a fine musician and her sister, Bay, was a professional violinist. Friends also called to play on their lovely grand piano, particularly Charles Lynch, a concert pianist confined to Dublin during these war years. The following year Gerard exhibited his pride in being allowed to work there and to reflect the fact that he was an accepted member of this community. Mainie also arranged for him to become a member of The Dublin Painters Gallery of which she was the first President in 1920.

Although dividing his time between Dublin and Belfast, it was in Belfast that he made lasting friendships. One of these was with Hugh Heanon who arrived in Dublin to stay with him and later shared his flat in Abbey Road in London. But his friendship with the Belfast painter, Daniel O'Neill, was to be one of the most significant for him in those years, as O'Neill was a most interesting artist with something of the same background as himself who was striving to make his way forward at a time when there was little interest for pictures in war-torn Belfast.

Daniel O'Neill had a cottage in Conlig, a Co Down village in the Ards Peninsula and local inhabitants remember what they describe as his artist temperament. Mrs Harry Monaghan has recalled that when there was a storm, Dan would go up to the hills at 2 or 3 o'clock in the early morning to watch for thunder and lightning. When she referred to this the next day Dan told her 'it was really beautiful with the lightning flashing through trees'. In fact all Dan's pictures have a curious electric tone of night blue which give a most romantic quality to the rather fey, round faced characters in his paintings. Gerard went to stay with him on several occasions in Conlig and Dan did a pencil sketch of him (page 37). They painted together and made several essays to sell their pictures in Belfast without much success. Later Gerard arranged an exhibition for them both in The Contemporary Painters Gallery in Dublin and this was opened by the distinguished architect, Michael Scott, in December 1943. A photograph of the time (page 40) shows them both standing in the gallery with Gerard's painting 'Sailors' in the background. Dan must also have been in contact with his future wife, Eileen, at this time for he included a painting of her in this exhibition. It was a large show, containing in all 70 works, and they both sold quite well. Gerard's paintings were still very dependent on places or persons of his everyday life; for example the picture 'Hedy Lamarr and Ginger Rogers' (page 42) reflected his undying passion for films, but it also showed a very adventurous application of thick textures of oil paint. He also began to exhibit pictures related to his mother's death like 'At The Wake' and shortly afterwards 'Dust to Dust' (page 25) touchingly concerned with youthful altarboys symbolic of his own childhood.

Gerard's relationship with Dan O'Neill was extremely important to him and he was deeply hurt when Dan married Eileen. They always kept in touch and Dan continued to attempt to renew this spiritual relationship, in spite of the fact that Gerard resisted his overtures, even to the point of pretending that he was not at home when Dan would call. The last time was shortly before Gerard died in 1971 and on that occasion force had to be applied to persuade Dan to leave. This was a most unhappy situation which reflected Gerard's strange psychological make-up. Like many other artistic characters, it appears that Gerard was a repressed homosexual, who by nature was drawn to men rather than women. However because of his formidable religious mother's upbringing, he could not permit himself to

partake in a life of sexual gratification which he felt contravened every aspect of the religious teaching she had drummed into him, but more particularly left him experiencing an intense guilt which made the other's presence intolerable.

These facts had already been confirmed by Pino Saglietti and subsequently by others of his friends with whom he had formed relationships. Nevertheless he kept many photographs of Dan in his album including cutouts which excluded all but his appearance. He seemed never able to exclude Dan's image from his subconscious and several later paintings (page 7) reflect that cast of countenance and tall figure.

In May 1943, Gerard and Dan had participated in the Golden Jubilee Exhibition of The Gaelic League in St Mary's Hall in Belfast. Gerard showed seven pictures and his sinuous almost abstract sculpture 'Slumber', whilst Dan showed only two works. This was a special occasion and pictures were invited from a group of distinguished older artists, like Paul Henry, William Conor, Morris Harding, S.R. Praeger, Charles Lamb and Letitia Hamilton and craft and needleworks were also included. Arthur Campbell and his brother George also exhibited at it. In a halfhour TV talk on the BBC in 1979, George Campbell spoke of this exhibition, 'I think I mentioned that I showed a drawing — for the first time — at a Feis in Belfast. This guy came over to me and said "I like your drawing. I'm Gerard Dillon." "Well, thank God," I replied "you are the one who did the big painting. You are the very man I want to meet. You can tell me how to buy brushes, paints, whatever I need, linseed oil ...." ' Thus began the longest-lasting and closest friendship of Gerard's life.

George and his wife Madge and Gerard really got on from the start and George used to call up to Clonard Street and the two would go out sketching together. On occasion they would go down in the evening with Dan O'Neill to a pub called Dubarrys, frequented by prostitutes and American soldiers, and here they would do quick sketches for the soldiers for little more than the price of a drink. Around about this time too they were invited to paint murals and scenery for Hubert Wilmot's Theatre in North Street. In fact Hubert Wilmot shortly afterwards moved his theatre to Fountain Street Mews. Nevertheless, George and Gerard had greatly enjoyed the experience of painting on a large scale and at last being free to really let go with colour. At this time George and Arthur Campbell were working for

Ginger Rogers and Hedy Lamarr, oil on canvas, 18" x 14", signed. Exhibited at Contemporary Picture Galleries, Dublin, 1943. PC

an exhibition to be held in Moll's Gallery in Queen Street in Belfast but they were all young and energetic and they refused no opportunities. In fact after finishing the Wilmot theatre they were invited to paint the bare walls of a barber's shop in Royal Avenue, in return for which they could show their pictures there. Shortly after this they were asked to exhibit their paintings in the Duke of York's pub in Commercial Lane, because the only art gallery then operating in Belfast was totally opposed to all forms of modern art. In reference to this fact Arthur Campbell recalls that at this time Dan O'Neill went into Magee's Gallery in Donegal Square West one day to look around. On being approached by the owner he showed the painting he had in a parcel under his arm. The owner turned pale when he saw it and said he was not interested and proceeded to turn out the gallery lights. O'Neill's reaction was one of total despair. He walked out onto the street, took his painting out of its wrapping and holding it upright on the pavement, proceeded to kick it along; each time it just landed on the ground he gave it another unmerciful kick until he had 'belted it into smithereens', and went on his way having given satisfaction to his artistic frustration.

Apart from having shared the Dublin exhibition with Dan O'Neill, Gerard could look back on the year 1943 in Belfast with a feeling of satisfaction. He had greatly expanded his artistic contacts and shown in a number of venues, and in the Spring exhibition of The Royal Hibernian Academy in Dublin his 'Disused Brickfields' was accepted. He felt particular satisfaction about this because it was a well-advertised fact that the selection committee of the academy demanded a standard related to quality of drawing and execution rather than to originality of subject. Later that year, at its inaugural, the Irish Exhibition of Living Art included three of his oil paintings, 'Black Eyes', 'Crucified City' and 'Cemetery Sunday'. He thus was the first Belfast artist of the younger generation to have made his mark in Dublin and he could feel with some certainty that he had at last arrived.

The Cottage Window, oil on board, signed, 16" x 20", circa 1944. Exhibited Lewinter Brankl Collection, Belfast Museum and Art Gallery 1958. PC

6. Wartime and After

In 1943, Arthur and George Campbell had produced a little book which was principally aimed at publishing Ulster artists and which consisted of sixteen pages of drawings by themselves, Patricia Webb and Maurice Wilks. This they called 'Ulster in Black and White' and as it was well received they decided to expand it the next year and produced 'Now in Ulster'. This was a magazine of short stories, articles and poems together with reproductions of paintings, photographs and thumbnail sketches. Their writers included a group who were to become distinguished in the years ahead, John Hewitt, W.R. Rodgers, Sam Hanna Bell, Denis Ireland and Roy McFadden, amongst others. The quality of the writing and pictures included was extremely high and carries a nostalgic recall of a regional character and intimacy, which perhaps dimmed a little at the conclusion of the war in 1945 when an urge to modernism dominated the minds of artists in all media. Amongst the paintings reproduced were three of town scenes by George Campbell, Daniel O'Neill and Gerard Dillon respectively. The Campbell 'Dead Street' is a flickering, impressionist study and the O'Neill 'Conlig Street' is a series of moody, impasto surfaces suggesting his romantic method. Dillon's 'Bombed Street', though structured in the same kind of surfaces as O'Neill's, picks out the shapes of the lamppost, the ruined houses and the caricatured figures bearing their salvaged goods. To make the picture was the primary object of O'Neill and Campbell, whereas the human predicament and the destruction obsessed Dillon. Summing all this up in his brilliant essay, John Hewitt, poet and curator of the Ulster Museum and Art Gallery, wrote 'O'Neill is more deeply subjective than Dillon or Campbell. Campbell comments on things and events. Dillon makes his little world out of hints his senses convey from the visible world'.

Hewitt contrasted the painting of John Luke, a classicist and Colin Middleton, a surrealist with that of O'Neill, Campbell and Dillon. Of them he says 'They aim at and succeed in responding immediately to the joy and pity of their days. More often to the pity. The pity for the shabby, the hopeless, sometimes shocked into the violence of the street accident or the air raid. It is therefore no mere chance that Campbell and Dillon are here represented by pictures of the Blitz, surely the event of our time with the harshest impact — at any rate for those of us who have not fought.'

He goes on to say 'The question of scale applies in a way to Gerard Dillon who, like Campbell is rather prone to exhibit his notes, or to work on areas too restricted to allow for the complete carrying out of his idea. In common with Campbell, too, he shares response to pity and pathos — the crumpled house, the shawled evacuee, the Sister of Mercy in the roaring street; with this difference, that although the handling has the same chancy, dashed-off quality, there is a certain sense of affection communicated, as if he loved his people and the places where they live. One might say, if it is not too soon to generalise about men who in years or experience cannot be expected to have reached maturity, that Campbell is a vivid commentator, some of whose comments are surprising in their rightness, while others are too slight to bear intense scrutiny; in any case "a chiel amang ye takin notes"; but Dillon is the maker and manipulator of a mannikin world; the little shuffling people in the little ruined streets have their own vitality and validity. Dillon too, has the same unfenced fertility, the same danger of superficiality. His colour is however, more cheerful, more lyrical. The distortions in Campbell are frequently the result of chance; in Dillon they tend to be romantic rather than organic, that is to say caused by feeling rather than by the structural necessities of the problem. His work has improved rapidly in recent years. He has succeeded in shedding much of his indebtedness to Picasso — the Picasso of the acrobats — and of the huge, goofy classical figures; an indebtedness which seemed to me to be to black and white reproductions chiefly rather than in colour. At times, however, he is capable of charming pastiche.'

Gerard and George Campbell were working at this time for an exhibition which was arranged in the gallery of John Lamb in Portadown. John Lamb was a brother of the painter, Charles Lamb, who settled in Connemara which area was to be his lifetime's subject, and the gallery largely existed to exhibit his works. They each showed 10 oils and 20 watercolours, but sales were not very good. Gerard had become very friendly with

Above: *Island People,* oil on canvas, signed, 16"x21". Exhibited Victor Waddington Galleries, Dublin 1953. Crawford Municipal Art Gallery, Cork.

Previous page top: *Gentle Breeze,* tapestry stitched by hand by the artist. Exhibited IELA 1953. Bord Fáilte, Dublin, Irish Tourist Board. Bottom: *A Mountain Farm,* oil on panel, 11¼"x14", signed, circa 1950. PC. Page 46 bottom: *Seaweed Man,* tapestry stitched by Aggie White from the artist's cartoon, 25"x19", 1954. Aggie and James White.

Page 45 top: *Irish Peasant Children*, oil on canvas, 14"x12", signed, circa 1949. Exhibited Institute of Contemporary Art, Boston 1950. PC. Page 45 bottom: *Lobster Pots,* oil on board, 20"x24", signed. Exhibited IELA 1951. PC.

Nano Reid, who lived and worked from her parents' public house and lounge bar at the entrance to the town of Drogheda. She invited Gerard to stay and they both painted on the banks of the River Boyne. Nano (1905-1981) was a more expressionist painter than Gerard and was held in high esteem by the adventurous artists and collectors in Ireland. Several of Gerard's pictures in the Portadown exhibition featured the Boyne area and of course Monasterboice, the sixth to eleventh century monastery, and the Cistercian Abbey at Mellifont and he was gradually to absorb into his subjects a feeling of this antiquity as well as the remoteness of that wild scenery which appealed to him.

He had visited the Aran Islands earlier that year and his 'Potato Pickers' (page 51) was among three pictures which were chosen for the 1944 Irish Exhibition of Living Art. In works like this, one can observe him departing from his former preoccupation with anecdote and reportage and moving into the area of a central subject. The young man encircled by the little stone wall which had been painfully erected by the farmers of the past in order to clear the earth within, both to give sustenance for the vegetables and to give protection from the frequent Atlantic storms, repeats the age-old story of life on remote islands like Aran. Outside are carefully placed animals, a cottage, a man and a small tree and by their scale they work to centralise the young potato picker. By absorbing the human forms into the patterns of the place, Dillon finds a new means of forming his style towards the rhythm which belongs to that landscape.

Earlier that year Arthur and George Campbell had held an exhibition in the gallery of William Moll & Son, 54 Upper Queen Street, Belfast and arising from that a new group of painters banded together to put on an exhibition at 48 Upper Queen St. They were Dan O'Neill, George Campbell, John Turner and Gerard Dillon. These artists were also included in another exhibition in August/September of that year organised by the newly formed Council for the Encouragement of Music and the Arts (CEMA) and three works of Gerard's were included in it.

Altogether Gerard spent much time in the family house in Lower Clonard Street in those war years. He seemed to be charged with an energy for painting and he painted all the walls of the house white like the Connemara cottages, and on the walls of the kitchen and staircase he painted a series of double heads influenced by the stonecarvings he had seen in the West. He even painted the blinds on the kitchen window and the children would stand outside in the dark evenings when the blinds were pulled down and pretend they were at the picture house. Even these images on the blinds (page 6) have a monastic feeling as if he wanted to reflect the concept of the stained glass windows in churches when seen from the outside.

His mind was deeply affected by the sense of Ireland's past which stonecarvings like those at Monasterboice and the 4,000 years-old decorated stones at Newgrange Tumulus invoked in him when he visited them with Nano Reid on his painting sessions earlier. The figures contained in them, however blunted by the centuries of weathering and formalised by the stonecarvers' techniques, seemed to him to match the curious air of simplicity which the inhabitants of Connemara took on as they worked in the crags and tiny fields of their farmlands or on the shores where they fished or gathered seaweed for the purpose of manuring the land. During these years, so formative in the growth of his style, it was his frequent visits to the West that gave him fresh stimulation and encouraged him to invent colour harmonies based on the red petticoat-type skirts worn by the girls and the black hats and white bawneens worn by the men. Gradually he was building up a method of representing the Western seaboard which totally differed from the earlier process of Paul Henry, Charles Lamb and their contemporaries; they concentrated on the overall landscape effects both of weather and vegetation whereas he picked out the little images of men and women at work, of horses and donkeys, goat and ducks and simplified them into symbols of the area as the carvers and illuminators of the past had done. Like them he made thumbnail sketches on the spot and later he floated them with paint into his pictures.

A little sketch called 'Threshing in Connemara' dated 1944, though extremely simple, is a good example of the method he adopted towards the creation of these paintings which were to make his work distinctive during the coming years. He had become adept at capturing the gestures and significant movement of people in characteristic poses by making these little thumbnail sketches, and five of them were reproduced in 'Now in Ulster' published in 1944. He seems always to have used this method of recording impressions and putting them by for later introduction to his pictures. Sometimes in discussion with this writer, when words failed him to project an image in his mind, he would pick up a pencil and with a couple of flourishes would illustrate it perfectly.

In the early Spring of 1945 he was introduced to an agent of P.J. Walls, the London builder who was recruiting men to go over to London to do emergency repairs to bombed housing sites. A party was set up consisting of Cyril Murray, Paul Lynas, and Charlie Kelly with Gerard as a sort of ganger or leader because he knew London well, had worked there as a house painter in the thirties and was quickly able to take up the ideas of the agent. All they needed was travel identity cards to gain entry to London.

Cyril Murray has described to me how they were provided with a flat in the Prince Albert Road, just overlooking the Zoological Gardens in Regent's Park, which the authorities had commandeered for emergency workers. Their first job was in Ponder's End and here they set to work to replace slates and windows and clear up the rubble and mess in the rooms. They were paid on a time and material basis.

> We were a flying squad, [Cyril told me]. Houses would be damaged by blast, windows blown in and chaos created. Our job was to make the place habitable once again. The fact that Gerard was there ensured that the work was done. He was able to hold us together and guide us. He was very conscientious. He would not allow himself to be called a foreman but he kept us at it. I was only 17 at the time. It was my University. Gerard was the oldest of us, secondly he was most experienced and he was a natural leader. We all loved him — he was an immensely popular chap and we looked up to him. He was a sort of keystone. When there were rows and disputes he would settle them. He was in his late twenties but he never looked as old as this. He was terribly young in his attitudes. Interminable arguments and discussions went on about art, religion, literature and politics. Our life there was one long debate. Others overhearing our discussions probably thought we were having flaming rows but it was our Northern Irish way of conversing. Two of our group were very literary minded. Paul Lynas, the son of a clergyman, was very sensitive and Charlie Kelly who wore a little beard wrote poetry. So there was no lack of subjects to discuss. And I, like Gerard, was very anti-religious and was always looking for more information. Then another Northern Irish chap, Paddy Kelly, joined us. He was a friend of Gerard's from his former time in London. He was a talker, articulate and a strong personality whom Gerard greatly liked.

Sometimes Gerard would read chapters from a book and he would take three or four parts, changing his voice each time if he was reading a play. He was fascinatingly entertaining and we bemused him. But he also had his own private life and friends and sometimes would go off on his own. Eventually he set up his own accommodation and ceased to live with us. One by one the group found places to live privately though they stayed together as far as the work was concerned.

Sometime later Cyril Murray fell in love and decided he would get married. His fiancee, though not a Catholic, agreed to get married in a Catholic church and set about making the necessary arrangements. Gerard was to be best man. So Cyril and Gerard went to meet the priest in Kensington where the marriage was to take place.

> When we arrived, we walked into the church, [said Cyril] and Gerard looked around him and then he said to me 'and what are you doing here. This is not a bloody Catholic church, it's a bloody Anglican church.' I explained that the priest was called Father and that he wore a soutane etc., and it all looked the same. So I asked him to come and meet the priest; because of course I couldn't care less myself. He said 'your mother would have a fit if you got married here. We must go and get a proper Catholic church.' When I told my fiancée, we called the whole thing off for six months. But we did eventually get married in a Catholic church but Gerard was not the best man as he had gone back to Belfast at the time.

It seemed as if Gerard accepted totally all the rules and regulations of his mother's world, both of religion and nationalism, in spite of the fact that he took no part in the activities of the church or of the political communities. But firmly fixed in his mind was a rigorous adherence to his mother's ideals and principles and he remained uncompromising in his loyalty to them.

The involvement in the building rehabilitation work kept him fully involved for almost all of 1945 with the result that he was not represented at all in the Irish Exhibition of Living Art that year. His sister Molly had acquired a house earlier at 102 Abbey Road, London, N.W.6 and he moved in as a tenant, converting the basement into a flat which had its own independent entrance. He was to live here, on and off, for the next twenty years and shortly after the end of the war, many of his Belfast friends were also to find accommodation there. His friend Hugh Heanon moved in immediately and occupied the second bedroom in the flat, thereby sharing

Above: Potato Pickers, oil on panel, signed, 16" x 24". Exhibited Irish Exhibition of Living Art 1944. PC
Below: The Spectator, oil on canvas, 12" x 20". Exhibited Victor Waddington Gallery, Dublin 1950. PC

the rent which he paid to Molly, was a most thrifty and hardworking woman who eventually paid off the mortgage on the house.

Gerard felt that as Molly was occupying the top part of the house and as he was in the basement with two complete floors between them, he would have a reasonable amount of privacy. However, there was Molly's concern for his welfare and her long-standing feeling that he was her special baby-brother; acting as substitute mother was not an emotion she was ever able to suppress. Furthermore she was the complete bachelor woman with an unusual affection for animals, cats, dogs and any stray birds on whom she could lavish her emotions. Accordingly she soon arranged an outside life, consisting of a wicker basket and a rope with which she would lower her cats and dogs from her window down into the garden below where Gerard, alerted by the loud ringing of her gong, had to emerge and release the animal in question. When the toilet activities had been completed he would replace it in the basket and Molly would haul it back up. This became a matter of great amusement to the neighbours and to Gerard's visitors and at times also a considerable irritation to him.

About this time, [Pino Saglietti told me] Molly found a little wounded bird in the gutter which she dearly wished to bring back to health. In order to take some rest from her constant care of it she asked Gerard to take it down to his flat overnight and to get up from bed every hour in order to give it food. 'So I went into the garden', Gerard said, 'and I got some worms and I used to feed it with a match-stick. Then I thought — it's not nice to have these worms alive in the room; so I fried them up with some butter and every hour I had to set my alarm and I'd get up to feed this little bird. Then during the night the match-stick disappeared. So I called up Molly and told her that the bird had swallowed the match-stick. She said 'Oh my God, it will die. We must get it to the Vet. immediately.' At four o'clock in the morning, the two of us went to the Vet. with the bird and told him that the bird had swallowed the match. 'Look here,' said this Vet. — 'I'm taking this bird. I'll look after it but please do me a favour, the next time you see an animal of any sort, look the other way.' Gerard told me the next day that he was worn out, and I said 'You know birds want to sleep too,' and Gerard replied 'Well the bird opened its mouth for food every hour when I got up.'

Pino also told me that Molly left the front door open every day, so that the cats could come and go. When Pino told her how inviting for burglars this was she replied 'Well, it's their home and I must look after them.' Pino's mother took Molly on a holiday to their home in Italy. The spent a month there as soon as the war was over. Pino's mother said 'It was a wonder she wasn't imprisoned. When we would go to a restaurant to have tea and cakes, Molly would feed the cakes to the stray dogs.' When his mother protested, Molly said 'The children have mothers and fathers, the dogs haven't.' Finally Pino told me 'And the people out there still remember her after all those years.'

In May 1954, Gerard's father died and he returned home to Belfast. At this time Joe was looking after the house in Lower Clonard Street as Anne had gone off to the USA to get married. Gerard always felt ashamed that he had so little feeling for his father. This was due no doubt to the general situation that had grown up over the years between his parents. While he was at home, CEMA arranged a one-man show of his pictures in Belfast, but apparently no catalogue was made at the time. Almost all of the pictures reflected his visits to Connemara. In the same year in Dublin The Irish Exhibition of Living Art were unable to obtain the gallery where they normally displayed their work and they consequently arranged with the Leicester Gallery in London to bring over the exhibition there. This was a very important occasion for Irish artists, reflecting as it did the activity which had taken place in Ireland during the war years when London life had been so disrupted. Parallel with this the Leicester Gallery featured an exhibition of sculptures and drawings by Henry Moore, who by now had become recognised as one of the world's leading sculptors. The Living Art exhibition contained 72 paintings and 4 stained glass panels by Evie Hone. Four of Gerard's pictures were included, 'Aran Funeral', 'The Well', 'Dust to Dust' (page 25) and 'Couple from Inishman'. The press reported most favourably on the show and recorded that one third of the works were sold in the first three days. This occasion did much to establish Gerard's position in London as an accepted painter of Western Irish scenes which captured certain simple but direct qualities of the people there, whose way of life had been virtually unaffected by the devastating war just concluded.

Gerard had given up his work on the building sites to leave himself free to visit Connemara once more, but he painted a number of pictures in London from the quick sketches he had made during this period. One of the most complete of these was 'Demolition' below, in which he almost totally ignored the shape of the house, apart from its compartmented values, rather reminiscent of his Irish scenes broken up by the small stone walls. As this time his work in reconstructing sites had encouraged an interest in the conception of houses without fronts so that he could contrast the rooms and their contents and occupants seen from the standpoint of a doll's house open for a child to play. 'The New Building' and several such pictures as 'Demolition' followed this principle. He was to elaborate this idea also in some of the Western

scenes like 'The Spectator' (page 51), painted at this time but not exhibited until 1950, in which his love of anecdote could be combined into a more complete composition taking on the realism of the landscape. The stone walls around the road and the four fields provide him with the means to suggest that the goats locked head-on reflect the bull-fight. But the extremely static quality of the human figures recall the medieval Celtic Crosses rather than the house interiors with the labourers actively involved in reconstruction.

Demolition, oil on canvas, 24" x 20", signed, circa 1950. Exhibited Dawson Gallery 1959. PC

7. Into the New World

The success of the Irish exhibition in London in the autumn of 1946 led to an invitation being issued to a group of these painters by the Associated American Artists' Galleries in 5th Avenue, New York. Opening the exhibition on 3 March 1947, Reeves Leventhal, their President, said that 'Contemporary Irish paintings had become known throughout Europe. It is therefore fitting that the first exchange exhibition be a representative collection of Irish pictures.' Writing about the exhibition Dr Theodore Goodman stated that 'the subject matter is typically Hibernian in its poetic often mystic quality. One example of this is Gerard Dillon's "Turn your Money" which shows two women looking at the new moon over their left shoulders. It is done in somber, quiet tones in direct contrast to the splashy colours characteristic of the veteran Jack Butler Yeats paintings.' Later the exhibition was shown in Chicago, Washington and Los Angeles.

From this time forward the modern group of Ulster artists became established in the public mind as a special aspect of post-war Irish art which had turned away from academic standards and moved into new areas of individuality. The Victor Waddington Galleries in Dublin later in 1947 put on an exhibition of works by Campbell, Dillon and O'Neill from Belfast and of Neville Johnson, an English artist who had settled there. This received most favourable reviews. The writer Benedict Kiely wrote 'Gerard Dillon's twelve paintings, I overheard described as the only "Irish" work on view. What the overheard speaker meant was that Gerard Dillon, except in one picture of Hampstead Heath under snow, looked for his material in the accepted way among the playboys of the Western World.'

I myself was art critic for the *Irish Press* at the time and wrote that 'Gerard Dillon has taken the people of Aran in their Sunday costumes and rendered them into decorative groups after the manner of Christopher Wood. This is sheer stage-Irish if viewed from the realist angle. But considered from the point of view of colour and design it is sheer charm.

After all is it not just as valid to romanticise the costumes of the West as that of Venice or Rome? In any case Gerard Dillon should be engaged on the wall paintings of the next public building in Ireland for which the luxury can be afforded. Meanwhile he gives one to sing and to laugh at his merry inventions.' He apparently felt hurt by my use of the term 'stage-Irish' although I was really emphasising how he used the costume to give decorative value to his pictures. Sometime later in an Irish review *Envoy* No 15, Feb. 1951 he wrote:

Sean Keating's illustrations for 'The Playboy of The Western World' and the pictures of Marc Chagall were the first things that made me want to paint.

Some Irish critics have said that I'm 'stage Irish', that I see the people and the landscape of the West with the eye of a visitor. Think of the West and the life lived there. Then think of my childhood and youth in the middle of industrial Belfast. Is not the West and the life there a great strange land of wonder to the visitor from the red brick city? I suppose these critics call Synge 'stage-Irish' and deny that his work is art.

The Irish are a nation of talkers and storytellers. It follows that most of her artists are literary in their approach to painting. Difficult it is for us to be anything else. Listen to us sing, the words are more important than the tune. We sing dozens of songs about dozens of men fighting and dying on hillside and in glen. How they went out on one summer's morn, or cold December day, with a brave young heart and spirit that knew no fear. And even after the bullet has laid him low, we go on and on to tell how the sweetheart or brokenhearted mother came to weep and pray in the valley, or on the bridge, or on the hillside. We all love it and why shouldn't we?

The Irish painter is trying to fight this storytelling quality (natural in himself) in his work, because he knows it isn't 'Pure painting'. It's a hard fight.

Gerard's confession that the painter has to fight the story-telling quality in his work because he knows that it isn't pure painting is a clear indication that he was concerned at the time that he was too dependent on the literal translation of the Connemara people and their surroundings into his paintings. By stating that it was not pure painting he was apparently reacting to the growing preponderance of abstract painting in the art world of Europe and America, in which the artist moved ever further away from the exact image and instead confected surfaces of paint-textures and colours which contained no image or if it did, it was up to the viewer to find it below the surface, rather than be confronted with it in the traditional way.

One of the outlets for his desire to be less literal was his use of the Celtic stone cross which he sometimes adapted to the subject on which he was working. He gradually evolved this method having directly painted these crosses and then by clever re-arrangement of parts of them he suggested the life of some of those portrayed within them. 'The Community' for instance is a rectangle in two sections. On the right two monks stand holding hands, side by side. Their hair and beards are arranged in the sweeping curls of the Celtic manuscript illuminator's style and their garments are decorated with human motifs expressing the artist's sense of fun. On the left in three sections are shown the monks in bed, on top and at the base praying over a coffined figure. In the centre they are shown at dinner around the table with fish on their plates.

He succeeded in 'The Community' in creating a consciously primitive or naive variation of the combined styles of early manuscripts and stonecarvings created by Irish monks of the period from the seventh to the tenth century. By his deliberate use of the breadth of method of the stonecarvers he was able to translate the fine line of the illuminators into the painterly style he was employing. He also painted 'Fast Day' (page 56) in this manner, using animal motifs for the marginal decoration and showing the monks around the table with Celtic designs on their costumes which enabled him to introduce very painterly brush strokes and to make his picture sing with this translated Celtic harmony, stolen from the first millennium and treated in his broad brushstrokes of the 1950s period.

He adapted this mannerism in to many works of a more creative kind. One such is filled with a romanticism and tenderness and shows two young men, one seated on the seashore, one asleep on top of a stone tomb or sarcophagus, reflecting the sculpture usually placed on such tombs in cathedrals. Behind, the moon is a white disc over the sea. 'Grey Beach' (page 56) he called this work and used another stone coffin, greatly reduced in size, in the foreground on the left of the young man's hand, with the image of a naked woman carved thereon. The stone tomb above is decorated with three carved male figures, flanked by dogs and goats.

The two young men in 'Grey Beach' may well be the subjects of two other pictures of this period, 'On the Beach' (page 57) and 'The Cottage Gable' (page 57). In both of these he departs from the kind of treatment reflecting

Celtic sources and shows the young men dominant in scale and protagonists, so to speak, by the relationship of their forms and their withheld interest the one in the other. Are they, in fact, a couple he observed during his summer visits and into whom he projected something of his own imaginative desires, reflecting his own inhibitions by the degree of separation between the couple in all three pictures? Perhaps they reflect the sense of loneliness and isolation which he was to carry with him throughout his life and as a result of which he was never to have an intimate companion in his maturity.

It was rare for him to use a flat ground like the sand in 'On The Beach' or the whitewashed walls in 'The Cottage Gable'. No doubt this was to emphasise the suppressed interest which he created by his placing of these figures and the fixity of their gaze.

In these pictures Gerard captured much of the simple life and atmosphere of Connemara. The translation of Celtic rhythms of a bygone age fitted in easily because life was so little changed by the passage of time, or perhaps timelessness was not inappropriate in the scenes he chose to place his figures; no doubt also because he desired to relate the great period of Celtic art to that part of Ireland he had designated to become his land of heart's desire and symbol of ideal nationhood, far removed from the strife and turmoil between North and South.

This concept is summed up in the 'West of Ireland Landscape' (page 59) recently acquired by the National Gallery of Ireland. It actually includes one of the Celtic crosses and is a clear indication of how he was following a process on which he had decided. In the 'Acquisitions 1986-88 catalogue', Adrian Le Harivel points out that 'The flattened perspective and silhouetted figures (perhaps an allusion to the three ages of man) give a votive feel to the scene, with its curious details of a sculptured monk in the centre and oversize hens. Few details can be precisely identified, though the High Cross is similar to Muiredach's at Clonmacnoise. The artist is more concerned to show the harmony between the natural and man-made landscape with reference to things that are typical of the place. He employs simple outlines and sharp colour contrasts and likened these pictures to scenes on high crosses and insular manuscripts, which he made sketches from.'

He painted many pictures in this particular manner over the next few years such as 'St

Opposite top: *Fast Day*, oil on panel, 63" x 75". Exhibited IELA 1950. Drogheda Corp. Museum & Library
Opposite bottom: *Grey Beach*, oil on canvas, 20" x 24". Exhibited Victor Waddington Galleries 1950
Above: *The Cottage Gable*, oil on panel, 14" x 19", signed, circa 1950. PC
Below: *On the Beach*, oil on canvas, 12" x 18", signed, circa 1950. PC

Francis', for whom he had a special affection, and though that saint had nothing to do with Ireland he 'Celticised' him with the rhythms of his brush strokes and the birds and animals with which he surrounded him. His mother had given him 'Francis' as a first Christian name and the idea of treating 'St Francis' with illustrations of Irish origin no doubt appealed to his sense of humour. (See page 17.)

Once he had developed the process of breaking up his subjects into sections separated by enclosing lines, he became bolder in his approach and was prepared to include half-a-dozen scenes in a theme such as 'Imaginary Bride' (page 60) in which colour was a satisfactory divider of the separate parts laid out against a group of thatched cottages in the background. In this work, fascinating because of the difficulty of interpreting its meaning, one sees a mourning couple on the left, a woman and child in the centre and the Bride, eyes closed as she is encircled by the man, unlike the usual Connemara male. Indeed the artist may be implying that he is a Spanish sailor as tradition claims that Spanish sailors came ashore from time to time and fathered local children. The young boy asleep and the dead bird no doubt belong in the realm of superstition. Certainly the large crow behind, twice the size of the cottage on which it is perched, is certainly an ill omen. All of these elements are smoothly painted against the landscape with little respect for scale and perspective, but nevertheless making a bold and imposing effect much in the manner of Marc Chagall from whom Dillon himself admitted influence and he may have been reflecting an Irish use of that artist's Russian themes of marriage.

In the summer of 1947, Pino Saglietti invited Gerard to come to Italy and to stay in his family place of Borgotaro up in the mountains in the North. It was Gerard's first visit to the European mainland and he was fascinated by the Italian way of life though he had glimpsed something of this with the Sagliettis. The very intimate way the native Italians congregated in restaurants on Sundays and such occasions and their jollity and uninhibited enjoyment of life seemed strangely in contrast with his Irish upbringing. For though he had separated himself from home for a good part of the previous thirteen years he was still spiritually his mother's son and thought along her lines. They paid visits to Florence, Lucca and Parma during their month away and Pino went to pains to expose Gerard to the great treasures of Italian art and architecture. But without success. Pino was particularly annoyed when in the Pitti Palace, Gerard turned to him and said 'I can't be bothered with all those old things. I am only interested in the world around me and the people in it. Anyhow I can't paint in Italy, everything is too bright and gleaming.' However when they returned to the mountains he was able to work and he said to Pino 'Borgotaro is not Italy, it's Ireland up the hills.'

As Yeats had said of Oscar Wilde, so too did Gerard 'enjoy his own spontaneity' and while he was never to lose his narrow provincialism, he was most careful to cultivate his inner vision and to continue recording his impressions of everything he saw for further use in the creation of his pictures.

In the Irish Exhibition of Living Art he showed three of his Italian pictures: 'Italian Washerwomen' (page 61) was no doubt built up from his pencil sketches sharply defining the way the women lean across the big water tank and gossip away with the local village in front. His 'Memory Pool' (page 5) gets to grips with the movement of the people in the fields and the panorama behind. His main subject here is the woman bearing a basket on her head on the road in front of the pool in which is reflected a young man about whom the artist suggests she is dreaming as she walks along. He exhibited this picture much later but changed its title to 'Italian Harvest Scene', perhaps because of the resemblance of the young man in the pool to Daniel O'Neill which had found its way into his Italian reverie.

During the years leading up to Gerard's second Dublin one-man show in the Victor Waddington Gallery in 1950, his paintings were exhibited widely and they appeared in exhibitions in Belfast, London, Rotterdam and Amsterdam. In his introduction to the C.E.M.A. Belfast exhibition in December 1949, John Hewitt referred to his life in London 'with occasional Continental journeys and on one or two brief interludes of return to Ireland. The innate sympathy has broadened to include a quiet humour; but a deep nostalgia for home now draws its symbols from his experience on the Aran Islands years ago. These represent for him an idyllic age peopled by peasants, tinkers and travelling showmen, in which a blatantly pagan apparition causes no more than lifted brows of surprise.' Later he refers to it as Dillon's 'Aran Arcady'.

Victor Waddington had taken a considerable liking to the four Ulster painters

West of Ireland Landscape, oil on canvas, 16" x 35", signed, circa 1945. Exhibited 'A Personal Choice', Belltable Arts Centre, Limerick 1981. The National Gallery of Ireland

he had shown in 1947 and eventually he made an arrangement to become their agent and to deal with their work in Ireland. He was accommodating in his approach and following the practice of certain international dealers offered them a monthly salary which he would subsequently deduct from the sales of their works. Inevitably this led in time to disagreements as the artists felt deprived when sales produced little or no profit since they had already received sums of money in advance. Eventually both George Campbell and Gerard Dillon found the arrangement unsatisfactory and called it to a halt but Daniel O'Neill, who at this time had moved to London, continued to avail of it and even after Victor Waddington had also transferred his business to London, he was able to sell most of his paintings through the Montreal branch of Waddingtons which was operated by members of the family in Canada.

The 1950 show in Waddingtons gave the Dublin public an opportunity to judge the more mature Dillon, now 34 years of age. Almost all the pictures included, reflected the frequent visits to Moyard, Roundstone and Inishlackan, an island near to Roundstone where he and George Campbell stayed and found fascinating for its wildness and the fact that it had no such signs of civilisation as goes with shops and the like apart from the rowboats which brought them back to the

mainland. The popularity the Connemara paintings achieved was reflected in the continuing demand for exhibition overseas. Six of his pictures were included in a group of five Irish Painters at Arthur Tooth and Sons Ltd., in London in the summer of 1951. Another three paintings were included by the Scottish Arts Council in Edinburgh and subsequently in Arbroath, Aberdeen, Dundee and Ayr. Amongst these was 'Medical Students' (page 28) which had previously been purchased by The Haverty Trust in Dublin and presented by that body to The Ulster Museum and Art Gallery. This is an amusing domestic interior, bright in colour and cleverly composed to suggest the furnishings and equipment of a Belfast boarding house of the period. Through all his work ran a thread of primitivism or naivety which he himself felt was a cherished possession. On one occasion when an outspoken friend said that he thought a child might have painted some of his pictures, that friend recalled that he looked really pleased and replied 'that is the greatest compliment you could pay me, I am always trying to see with a child's innocence and sincerity.'

It is interesting to observe that this style of naive observation and straightforward painted surfaces, contains no hint of overpainting or tonal adjustments to give an added sense of perspective or realism. Quite the contrary, his lifetime's output was to be marked by this

Imaginary Bride, oil on panel, 16" x 28". Exhibited Tooth's Gallery, London, 1951. Exhibited Victor Waddington Gallery 1950. PC

determination always to deal with his subjects as he found or discovered them. It was almost as if he delighted in certain arrangements or contrasts and he had no hesitation in endeavouring to make his pictures reflect the bare bones of the quality in those arrangements or contrasts that gave him this pleasure. His Italian paintings for instance are concerned with the same relationship of natives to their surroundings as were all his pictures of Connemara. When he went to Spain in 1951 with George and Madge Campbell no change occurred in his approach. In fact when he exhibited some of his Spanish paintings in a one-man show in the Victor Waddington gallery in 1953 a Dublin critic remarked that his 'Balcony in Tarragona' is 'a development from his "Medieval Irish Pattern" which brings a new life and colour to a design derived from the pattern on a Celtic Cross.' The same critic points out that his pictures of Western Ireland 'ignore perspective, realism and even the far-from-irksome restrictions of primitive paintings, in order to present a complete chronicle of island life in a comparatively small space, and are reminiscent in their decorative arrangement of details of tapestry.'

George and Madge Campbell made frequent visits to Spain where George was specially welcome in musical circles because of his gifts as a Flamenco guitarist who was most highly regarded by native specialists there.

When they persuaded Gerard to join them in 1951, Madge told me that 'We went overland, 3rd class rail, right through France and into Spain, — Barcelona to Tarragona, Valencia, Granada and on to Malaga.' The restrictions about security in Spain were still in force at that time. The soldiers came over and stopped them sketching and they found it necessary to go to the police and obtain a licence permitting them to paint. It was Gerard's only visit to Spain and it made a great impression on him for its painterly qualities. Unlike Italy he found the uneven terrain and the strong contrast of light and shade sympathetic to his style. Of course having dealt with the brilliant light of Italy he was now more prepared for southern European conditions. The Bullfight too, excited him, partly because of the balletic gestures of the Matadors and attendants and partly because of the thrust and power of the bulls — all this was compelling material for his sketchbook.

He was still deeply involved in his Western idyll for he had started a tapestry in 1950 in Roundstone and it took him three years before it was complete and could be exhibited in the Irish Exhibition of Living Art in 1953. It was entitled 'Gentle Breeze' (page 47) and it contained all the elements of people and their surroundings in Roundstone and Inishlackan coordinated into a delightful maze of shapes in the flat patterns of wool, onto the canvas base and all stitched painstakingly by himself over the years. Most modern painters and tapestry designers send their cartoons to the great tapestry factories to be woven there, but Gerard started his own in Roundstone, at a time when he ran out of painting materials and perhaps adequate cash; obtaining a large canvas base and able to acquire wool ends in different colours locally, he set out to master the handcraft practised in cottages around the world for many hundreds of years. This tapestry is 36" x 48" in size and represents a very considerable output of energy. However, all his life Gerard was fascinated by handcrafts of all kinds and delighted to adapt and invent and generally build the objects of furniture and domestic use with which he liked to surround himself. Shortly after 'Gentle Breeze' was exhibited my wife, Aggie, expressed her great desire to acquire such a work and he instantly got out his paints and designed one for her and instructed her how to carry it out. He drew the outline on the canvas and commenced the first couple of sections of stitches for her. It is entitled 'Seaweed Man' (page 46) and is one of

our most treasured possessions. Above all it represents the extraordinary artistic and innovative capacity of the artist who could produce a design almost at will.

While our 'Seaweed Man' is a small kaleidoscope of his Connemara images in tapestry, the large 'Gentle Breeze' is a major invention on Gerard's part. It is probably inspired by the classical use of the head of Zephyrus, whose breath propels the boats across the waters. The breath of Zephyrus becomes part of the line of the countryside, which falls away beneath the sea and rises up again on the left. John Hewitt, writing about it, stated that it contained 'the whole Dillon cosmography in happy and rhythmic extension', and almost every critic regarded it as the outstanding feature of that year's Living Art exhibition.

All this time his base was in Molly's house in Abbey Road, in London and he had from time to time to seek material jobs to help him to survive. He was selling a reasonable amount of work but the necessity to travel away from London in order to find the material he

Italian Washer Women, oil on canvas, 36" x 46", signed. Exhibited Dawson Gallery 1957. The Oriel Gallery, Dublin

required as source for his paintings was his major preoccupation. His needs were extremely simple and his way of life could hardly have been less expensive but the urge to get to Connemara was continuous. Sometimes he gave a painting or two in return for the use of a thatched cottage in Inishlackan and sometimes he paid rent. Occasionally, some London friends accompanied him, especially those with whom he shared his painting interests. In 1949 Alice West and Phil Rafferty stayed with him in Roundstone and Alice recalls how annoyed he was because she had not brought her sketch book. He considered that painters must work everyday and as he continued to show his petulance she finally got some cards and began to make sketches on them. He had become friends with Alice with whom he shared painting expeditions and she introduced him to 'The Bunch of Grapes', a Dickensian pub on the Thames at Limehouse which Alice was painting at the time, and the excellent picture she made there was exhibited in The Royal Academy and now hangs in the 'Bunch of Grapes'.

The following year George and Madge Campbell stayed with him and they began a lifelong friendship with the Irish author, Kate O'Brien, who had a beautiful house in Roundstone which she had purchased out of the earnings from the film of 'That Lady'. Nano Reid frequently accompanied him at other times. On one occasion when Gerard was rowing her back to Roundstone a storm arose and gave rise to an incident which enabled Gerard to indulge in one of his favourite acts of mimicry which no doubt was much exaggerated, although Nano, who was one of the most respected Irish painters of her time, was also noted for her ability to resort to somewhat unparliamentary language. In the event, Gerard would give a most hilarious impersonation of Nano, alternately on her knees on the floor of the boat beseeching the Blessed Virgin to save them and then jumping to her feet in terror and in a flow of unprintable words admonishing Gerard to pull harder on the oars. It was also in Roundstone that he first met some London friends, including Dr Maura McQuaid, who was also a painter and later attended classes at which he taught.

In 1953, he took a cottage in Moyard, a village on the road to Renvyle, and George and Madge Campbell and the sculptor Oisin Kelly accompanied him. This was a memorable visit for the painters because Oisin Kelly let them into some of the secrets of his trade, including how to model with papier maché, and for Gerard in particular it was a new method of raising a surface on the painting ground in order to give variety to his patterns. This, perhaps, led him to introduce collage to his pictures, which was of course the addition of pieces of paper, coloured or variegated and stuck on to the picture surface. This was not an unusual technique amongst modern painters but for Gerard, who had never attended art schools, all ideas had to be experienced in practice so that they could become part of his working knowledge. He was an inveterate experimentor.

Design for a Mural for a Mantlepiece with a gas fire, pencil and watercolour on paper, 6" x 18", circa 1956

8. Life in Abbey Road

The Belfast pianist, Tom Davidson, came to stay in 102 Abbey Road in the early fifties and in fact Molly rented him an upstairs room as Hugh Heanon was occupying the second bedroom in Gerard's basement flat. Gerard had first met Tom Davidson with his brother, Joe who had asked Tom to play some Britten songs which he was learning. Because of Tom's continuing interest and involvement in the Belfast art world he became one of Gerard's closest friends, and from that time on the house in Abbey Road was the meeting place for Belfast artists when in London and a number of them stayed there. When Hugh Heanon left, Tom McCreanor took his room and in 1957, Arthur Armstrong moved in. Then, shortly afterwards Hal Rice and his painter-sister Noreen set up a flat on the top floor which they occupied for a period. Arthur Armstrong had his room on the third floor where Molly also had her apartments and a Mrs Adams (not one of the circle) had the Hall-door flat, whilst Gerard's basement flat was the centre of the social life of the house.

They all used the famous bell installed by Molly to call Gerard to attend to the animals. Noreen Rice tells me that one would lean out of the window and nominate the person to be contacted. In the evening they would assemble in Gerard's flat and friends in London would perhaps join the soiree and discuss and read their works if they were writers. Gerard and George Campbell had developed a technique of mimicry and recitation from the writers they both admired in the Theatre. The most famous of these were Ionescu, Beckett and Genet, whilst they also recited directly from Amanda McKittrick Ros and from Eric Cross's 'The Tailor and Ansty' because it seemed to evoke their summers in Connemara. They also made tapes from some of these which still exist, though modern tape machines are not responsive to the early techniques they were using at the time. Both Gerard and George and Madge Campbell had good voices and about that time Gerard contributed to a record for Pye Group, NPL 18028, with Ottiline Patterson, which is even now occasionally used on radio programmes to recall 1950's customs and ways. This is called 'Ottiline's Irish Night' and the songs Gerard sang were 'Cailin Deas' and 'I Know My Love'.

Among the Irish writers who visited the group and read from their work in progress were Aidan Higgins, Bill Naughton and Gerard Keenan. In Aidan Higgins' novel 'The Balcony of Europe' there is a chapter entitled 'Who's Paddy Kelly': he was part of the 'Bombed Sites' group in the last years of the war, with whom Gerard frequently drank and reminisced about Belfast life. Gerard had a habit of quoting Paddy Kelly to his friends. On pages 307/8 Aidan Higgins writes:

> The author is in his studio and was interrupted 'Is that you Paddy?' a voice asked. No, I said. 'Who is it then, bejasus?' the bowsy voice asked, and in came the homosexual housepainter, his voice raw from the morning air off the Quay.

There are further more explicit details further on in that chapter. Gerard Keenan was at this time engaged on a novel and one of the characters, Francie Gent, was clearly based on Gerard Dillon and contained criticism of his paintings. Indeed Gerard Keenan was a great admirer of Dillon's paintings and wrote the introduction to his one-man show in the CEMA gallery in Belfast in 1956. His novel was published as a serial in the 'Honest Ulsterman' in 1977/8 and it was entitled 'Farset and Gomorrah'. Farset represents Belfast and Francis was of course Gerard's first name which he did not use. The picture of Gerard as a person is not flattering, though he covers up the facts somewhat by describing him as a Dubliner, but there is an accurate description of his appearance from pages 84/5 of No 57 of the 'Honest Ulsterman', which reads:

> Gent was small and neatly dressed in very worn, much pressed, tweeds; neat also was his trim military moustache. He had a plump pale face and a plump pale bald head. His eyes were Chinese slits and twinkled as though they were wired to the mains. That he was homosexual was so obvious that a deaf man would have seen it in his dancing face and hands, a blind man heard it in his dancing accents. He looked poor and immensely self-confident. The night could have been described as very jolly, there was certainly much laughter, but Duggan was unhappy through it. Francie Gent had a fund of good stories, his anecdotes were witty and well delivered and often involved fairly famous writers, artists and actors; but his humour was relentless and Duggan felt intimidated, his jaws were sore from maintaining a serial ha-ha-ha, and he hadn't a single son-of-a-bitch anecdote to offer

tany or Tahiti looked inscrutable out of cottage interiors in the Arans or from horseback on their strands.
Gent dramatised his daily life in his paintings in the
way that his master had done, though with none of
Gauguin's self-pity and in a large, ambitious, successful canvas portraying multiple facets of Gent's London flat, a sort of massive bande-dessinée of One Day
in The Life of Francie Gent, the nude figure lying
face-down on his bed as a delicious reward at the end
of the day was the nude figure from the painting
Gauguin called Manao Tupapau.

This description of Gerard's flat referred to the
painting 'Self-contained Flat' (page 66) first
exhibited in the IELA in 1955 and purchased by
the Northern Irish Arts Council shortly
afterwards and now in the Ulster Museum. On
page 86 of this chapter, the author goes on to
describe this little garden flat as heaven and
stated:

> Francie had divided his living room with bookcases
> into foyer, sitting-room and bedroom. Furniture and

in return. But Francie Gent's paintings were so good
that Duggan decided to take up his invitation and visit
him in London.

Much Irish painting was landscape painted so square
that it looked as if it had been executed by
Wordsworth himself. When Francie Gent looked at
landscape he saw it filtered through a sensibility that
was steeped in Pont-Avon and Gauguin. He was a
child of the Dublin tenements, reared in Lower
Dominick Street, and his homelife had the classic
shape to favour the growth of homosexuality — an
intelligent, fiercely embittered mother and a weak,
drunken father. 'She kicked him out and never let us
speak to him again. Can you imagine, he was the local
bread man, but when he came to deliver bread in
Lower Dominick Street we had to come into the house
and stay there till he went past. "If I catch any of you
so much as smiling at your da, I'll kill you", she used
to say and she meant it. Then he died and we never
saw him again. She was awful hard and you can't
blame her. She'd all those children to rear and he spent
every penny he earned not so much on drink for
himself as standing drinks for all his hangers-on.'

Francie Gent got scant formal education, worked for
a living from an early age, hated intellectual talk, read
little. He saw Gauguin's work as a call to escape from
the educated in art, to return to primitive roots, which
was how Gauguin had seen it also. Gauguin's paintings of Breton calvaries became Gent paintings of
Celtic Crosses; Gauguin's celebration in flat, crude,
brightly coloured patterns of the poor fields of Brit-

Above: *The Yellow Bungalow*, oil on canvas, 30"x22". Purchased by the Thomas Haverty Trust 1954. Ulster Museum Belfast.
Opposite top left: ' *... That 'tis no plain priest you'll have to annoint you ...'* and *bottom left:* ' *... that you might have nicer legs than your own under your table ...'* Both are illustrations for 'Irish Blessings' by John B. Keane in *Ireland of the Welcomes*, vol. 17 no. 4, November–December 1968. Published by the Irish Tourist Board.

Above: *The Red Attic*, oil on board, 19½"x29½". Exhibited IELA 1953. Frances and Jim Ruane
Below: *Self Contained Flat*, oil on board, 48"x72", signed. Exhibited IELA 1955. Arts Council of Northern Ireland

Above: *Connemara Moon*, oil on panel, 18"x24", signed, circa 1957. PC
Below: *Kitchen Interior*, oil on panel, 30"x40", circa 1952. Radio Telefis Eireann Dublin

Above: *Whit Tuesday*, oil and sand on panel, 24½"x37", signed on rear 'Gerard Dillon '57'. Taylor Galleries Dublin
Below: *Any Old Irish Town*, oil on panel, 48"x72". Exhibited IELA 1958. PC

furnishings, carpets and curtains, were shabby, clean and colourful. The walls were covered with paintings, some framed, many unframed. The tools of Francie's trade were sitting around on mantlepiece and cupboard, and there they were also in the paintings on the wall. Duggan never tired of this effect, of looking from model to model's aesthetic reflection. If it was only a pair of pliers, a screwdriver and a blowlamp, their physical identity was glorified, dignified beyond measure, in the transcription to canvas.

The 'Self-contained flat' represented a move away from West of Ireland subjects into domestic scenes such as 'Red Attic' (page 66) and 'Yellow Bungalow' (page 65) which was purchased by the Thomas Haverty Trust and presented to the Ulster Museum, Belfast. They also represented something of the greater interest he was taking in the community life of 102 Abbey Road with his Belfast artist friends in residence and the constant flow of visitors with visual art and literary backgrounds.

The Belfast poet W.R. Rogers (1909-1969) had encouraged him to write more and had also invited him to take part in a programme on BBC Radio from Belfast on 23 December 1955 called the 'Return Room'; it was to centre around Roger's growing up in Belfast and set in poetical form. Gerard opened the programme singing 'My Lagan Love' for which George Campbell played the guitar accompaniment. Then Gerard recited three children's rhymes at the appropriate times. He also did a pencil sketch which was used to advertise the programme in the *Radio Times*.

He and George Campbell also got occasional parts in the chorus of the D'Oyly Carte Opera in London and they were paid nine shillings and sixpence for each night. They had the facility to adapt both to the music and

Above: Illustration for 'Walking the Farm' by Stephen Rynne in *Ireland of the Welcomes*, vol. 6 no. 2, July–August 1957. Published by the Irish Tourist Board.

characterisation, probably acquired over the years from taking part in the social evenings when the two of them were the ringleaders in organising the musical entertainment and persuading the shy members of the company to contribute.

Gerard was a most amusing entertainer and he was deeply loved by his circle of friends, many of whom were totally unaware of his homosexual lifestyle as described by Aidan Higgins and Gerard Keenan. W.R. Rogers, Bill Naughton the Belfast author and his wife, George and Madge Campbell, Tom Davidson,

Arthur Armstrong, Noreen and Hal Rice, and Cyril Murray of the Bombed Sites squad belonged to this group. One therefore has to conclude that he had a private world confined in a smaller circle which he kept quite separate from the majority of his friends in the world of art and in his family environment.

Though Gerard left a number of unpublished stories and articles and a one-act play called 'No Dotted Line for Me' together with the draft of another one-act play called 'Blue Nude, Blood Orange' amongst his papers, only one clear reference remains amongst those papers which refers to that private world. And though Aidan Higgins and Gerard Keenan are very explicit in their references, I have avoided quoting them fully as it is always difficult to draw a line between the actuality and the artistic licence used to give heightened value to characters in novels. However, since the poem in Gerard's papers has been typed and left with his other writings, it should perhaps be referred to. He called it 'The Rake's Progress' and it relates an occasion when he got a lift home on the pillion of a motor cyclist, who stayed the night with him. It ends by recording the sense of loneliness of following nights depending on a gas-fire for heat and company and makes a romantic expression of the situation of such men as he, whose lives are spent in continuous awareness of the sense of isolation to which there is no end if they share

Top and top right: Illustrations for 'Connemara is Ireland to me' written and illustrated by Gerard Dillon
in *Ireland of the Welcomes*, vol. 13 no. 2, July–August 1964. Published by the Irish Tourist Board.
Bottom: For 'The Dingle Peninsula' by Brian Fitzgerald in *Ireland of the Welcomes*, vol. 7 no. 3, Sept–Oct 1958.

Like the changing landscape, the local people change too. Old Seamus I met one evening hobbling along over the road made of shifting stones. He was all pink and aglow, with darting blue eyes. On each side sea stones rolled together to make a wall from his little house to the sea shore. All was pink, the sea a warm violet. Seamus was pink and his mood rosy too. He'd had a good catch that day. This old man lives near me and he is about eighty and although that he still stands over six foot high. Still he goes out fishing and works his little gardens; they are very small indeed, one has about three ridges of potatoes. He cuts his own turf from his own bog, and with a basket filled high on each side of the donkey he carries his fuel home to store for the winter. Six or seven sons he has, all cowboys in Oregon now, the youngest remains at home in a simple cottage with the plainest furniture. Straight hard handmade chairs. What with these chairs and these rough roads and rocky fields, it's no wonder these Western people are graceful and walk beautifully.

It's the difficulty to paint this place makes it so fascinating. It has so many aspects. It has so much to give. The fields are small and irregular, marked off by lace-like stone walls. Each field can be a different colour. A yellow field with a violet stone fringe, a brown field with a creamy white-border, an emerald one with a grey-green wall and so it can go on and on endlessly.

his inherited convictions. The importance of this aspect of his life on his artistic output gradually emerges both in his style and his subjects and no doubt is responsible for the very remarkable works of his later years.

It was at this period also that Bord Fáilte, the Irish Tourist Board, invited him to write and illustrate an article for their magazine *Ireland of the Welcomes*. It appeared in the May/June number 1955. He did this in the form of a letter with accompanying sketches and it begins:

Dear Reader, Connemara is the place for a painter. The stony parts are the parts for me. If you closed your eyes and suddenly opened them you'd think you'd been transported to the moon. It looks as if some strange gods had been playing stone-throwing games, like children do, with an old tin can as a cock-shot, until all around is strewn with stones. These god-like stones are huge boulders standing up all over the place, with here and there peeping behind them little cabins and long cottages, white, stark and elfin-like intruders in this strange stone world.

The light is wonderful here. Rocks, stones and boulders change colour all the time. Sometimes they are blue-green, other times pink, violet, creamy white and cool grey. Behind and around everywhere, the Twelve Pins tower up to the rolling clouds. They are forever changing colour too, one peak at a time, so that you can see at times a green peak, an orange-brown one, blue black, purple and grey peaks — it's terrific.

If his letter were not illustrated, it would still convey a painter's mind. He uses a most conversational tone to appeal to the reader in his personal way, and ends with this paragraph:

Bottom: Drawing on the cover of *The Artist*, vol. 52 no.2, issue 308, October 1956, indian ink on paper, 9" x 7", signed. *The Artist*, London W1. New York 14

One could live here forever but being neither a fisher-man nor farmer but only a painter, I'm forced to come back to city life to sell work — and hope to save enough to come back to Connemara. You don't know the wonderful holiday in store for you, over here. Why don't you come over and give your eyes a thrill? I hope you like the sketches. Yours, Gerard.

During coming years he wrote and illustrated many articles for *Ireland of the Welcomes* (see appendix 3) and he returned in the July 1964 edition to the same subject which he entitled 'Connemara is Ireland to Me'. In the course of this he wrote:

My numerous stays in Connemara have always been heaven, even when the bottom of heaven fell out and about us drenching everything around until the very grassblades flattened out and floated on the top of the flood racing through the fields to get to the sea. When the thatch leaked into bowls and basins, pouring like water from a shower-bath-rose out of order. Even these extremes have a beauty one doesn't get in the city or other more cultivated parts of the country. Happy carefree evenings spent in the company of artist friends, George Campbell and Oisin Kelly. As night fell we set out for a pub, Campbell bringing his guitar, and Kelly his fiddle, and there over a few 'jars' in a pleasant atmosphere we'd encourage the local people to sing and dance. Good singers you'd find and long forgotten songs re-living in the mellow light.

Written and illustrated by GERARD DILLON

These people are a race apart, very friendly and polite, they never intrude. They carry this politeness to a degree unbelievable to me, like the time when, as very amateur currachman pulling the oars with all my strength against a sea with a big swell on, finding the currach heading for a strange island instead of the one I called home. I remarked on this to my oar-pulling companion, a quiet islandman. 'Ah now it will be alright', says he. So I'm madly pulling on and on, tearing the back out of myself. And still the boat noses in the wrong direction, and me thinking 'if this keeps up we'll never get home this night'. After my third complaining enquiry he says 'Well it's like this, do you see, I didn't like to tell you, but like you see, you should be pulling very hard with the left arm and hardly at all with the right, if you do that from this time out we'll be home in no time'. So there he was putting a two-man effort into his pulling to counteract my city ignorance, ignorance he was too polite to tell me about. These people are strange, buried deep in themselves. If you have the gift you can draw them out and you might find another crock of gold. They are a people who like their freedom minute by minute, so that they can shy off any sort of responsibility even to themselves, very annoying to the bustler.

With all this literary activity, illustrating and painting, Gerard was still forced to take part-time jobs to survive financially and from 1953 to 1955 worked as a night porter in the English Speaking Union. Then in 1956 he was appointed as an art teacher at the Shepherd's Bush and later at Gloucester Road for a further five years. Perhaps the effect of having to teach and use models provoked him to break away from his Connemara subjects or perhaps he felt he had exhausted his inventive capacity in this area. He became totally excited by abstract painting and experimentation of various kinds. Many exhibitions were then being organised (see appendix 1) and he had an accumulation of paintings in stock and in fact had been moving away from his earlier style by the use of collage and other techniques like monotypes. During 1955 he was invited by the Editor of *The Artist* to contribute to this magazine which was widely circulated in the British Isles and the USA. In October 1956, the Editor used one of his Connemara drawings for his cover and wrote an editorial note about it stating:

Gerard Dillon especially portrays to us the very strong feeling he has for drawing. He feels that one should approach this subject with courage and conviction, and draw with clarity: firm and precise line. He pro-vokes his point with the group shown here where his strength of line is quite evident. Mr Dillon is an Irish artist, self taught. He has a most enquiring mind and spends a good deal of time experimenting with many

Illustration for opening page of 'Connemara is Ireland to me' written and illustrated by Gerard Dillon in *Ireland of the Welcomes*, vol. 13 no. 2, July–Aug 1964, pen on paper, 6" x 3½", monogrammed.

media separately and collectively. He will be writing a series of three articles for us on 'Unusual Media' in our next volume. He is a member of the selection committee of the most important exhibition in Ireland — The Irish Exhibition of Living Art — and his work has been widely shown in America, Germany, Holland and Finland. He has been well represented in Irish and American collections and in educational collections.

The three articles in question, illustrated and fairly lengthy, appeared in the issues of March, April and May of 1957. The first was on drawing and in this he, now as a teacher himself, had apparently come around to its importance and eating his earlier words states 'How dull we think; but all the while we are being taught to use our eyes, comparing as we go along the proportions of this against that, the ability to put objects in space one behind the other, until we have mastered perspective and use this knowledge automatically.'

'The Cupboard' (page 73) is reproduced in colour in the magazine and of it he writes that:

It is an example of one of my approaches to creating a pleasing composition. To begin with I took a colour reproduction of a stained glass window; an old English window. It was the centrepiece from some weekly magazine. After studying it well, I thought to myself, if I drew on top of this with ink I could make it a different picture. What to draw on top of it was the question. What did it lend itself to? After some time I thought the only thing that would fit the composition would be a cupboard. So I would destroy a window to make a cupboard. With a brush and Indian ink I drew crudely as I wanted to suggest an old dresser with old plates, cups, etc., enclosing the pieces of colour I wanted in my finished drawing. There is very little colour of my making in this picture. Examine the picture well. You will see two heads of angels in the lemons on the plate in the left corner of the bottom shelf. The top two plates have angels and part of their golden wings. The jug on the left has still got the hands of a saint and the red of some drapery. Then I took Chinese white to obliterate the parts I wanted to kill and also to heighten different parts of jugs, etc. The egg-cups were done with a wash of blue-green.

I would take any coloured reproduction and try to look at it as a multi-coloured page and not a picture, so that I might turn it upside down or on its side. By looking at it this way another picture may be suggested to me. The colour scheme or the drawing may give me a start. When I have got the idea in my head I take a brush and draw in my composition, using the lines and the masses of colour to help enliven my imagination. This is almost like looking for pictures in the fire, a pastime most of us have indulged in some time in our lives.

The last paragraph of the article reads:

This technique is surely one where you destroy something to create something different. Maybe it is a kink in my nature that I am never able to leave something as it is. Always wanting to change it, make it better or at least different; to transform it completely making something more to my liking. One of my childhood pastimes was cutting up pictures in magazines and newspapers and rearranging them into something else. Transplanting figures into impossible situations, taking animals from the quiet countryside, placing them into busy pictures of city streets and undergrounds. This habit led me later on to paper mosaics and collage. In my next article I will show you my results in this direction.

Amongst his papers, Gerard had a book of cutout photographs from magazines and these he rearranged by inserting pictures from other photographs in order to bring about amusing and unexpected combinations. He frequently placed important personages into impossible situations by giving them features or bodies totally unrelated to their lives and he would then retitle the work. One of these is reproduced (page 74) in order to show his method and though here he used the image of a British Prime Minister, his main interest was not so much vicious as comic and he never exhibited them or displayed them except as a social diversion for his friends.

In the second article for 'The Artist' he treated of collages in which process he was

The Cupboard, indian ink and collage on paper, 11" x 9". Reproduced to illustrate unusual media in *The Artist*, vol. 53 no.1, issue 311, March 1957

very adroit as a result of his playing with photographs and illustrations from an early age as a short cut to making pictures. He described this method thus:

> Take a sheet of stiff card or paper, the size depends on personal choice as does the colour. It can be either neutral or a definite colour. The semi-stiff backs of sketch books are very useful for this. Then draw your picture, composing very carefully. You need not be too fussy about the actual drawing, however, as later you will be doing the drawing on the pieces of coloured paper. All you need to do is to place your figures in the positions you want them. Or if it is a landscape, have the horizon and main structure of the houses, trees, etc., just exactly where you intend them. Then start selecting pieces of coloured illustrations.
>
> I usually keep a box with a variety of pieces already cut, so I just search through these for what I want and from then on it is like laying mosaic pieces together. By experience you will find your own method. We always end up by doing things our own way, and that is how it should be.

Further on he wrote:

> I used dark stiff paper like that used for pastel, when I started 'Mackerel Island'. This was a small island I once lived on, off the coast of Connemara in the West of Ireland. Small it was in every way; little cottages dotted here and there through its little fields; every inch of land seemed to have a stone wall around it. I wondered how I should approach this subject. I

thought small, moving patterns may give the feeling I have about the island — the feeling and sight of the moving planes one notices in a net full of living mackerel. So I decided on this broken quality. I again used dark grey paper as my base, roughing in the bit of land and the sea. I placed the pieces of coloured paper in a higgledy-piggledy way carrying this broken, moving idea even into the sky. When all was securely stuck down, I drew over this island pattern putting a little house here, a haycock there, a little man and dog, a few cattle, etc., until I was satisfied and felt right about what I had done. Then with a thin wash of light blue-grey gouache, I painted in the cracks left in the patterned sky. I feel this is one of the most successful of my 'collages'.

In the third of his articles on 'Unusual Media' he dealt with monotypes. This is a unique type of printing by which process it is only possible to obtain one print. Monotypes usually refer to prints taken from a sheet of glass. With his method of 'straight talk' he thus describes this medium:

> Take first a clean sheet of glass (thick glass is best as the thin is too easily cracked). The size of the glass will depend on personal needs — but do not use a sheet of glass just the desired length of the drawing — otherwise you will have no room to work. Next you will want a tube of lino ink — it can be oil or water colour — and a rubber roller. I, personally work very small, about 12 inches at the most, so that using a piece of glass about 20 inches by 16 inches I have ample room.

He then goes on to explain how to roll the ink on to the glass and placing a sheet of paper over it, the drawing is then done with a sharp pencil and when the paper is removed the pressure of the drawing has transferred the ink to the paper and a specialised kind of picture has been achieved.

Sometime previously he had painted a picture 'Moon over The Bog' which was sold at his first one-man show in America at the Maxwell Galleries in San Francisco. At the time he was unable to get the moon to reflect that totally different texture from the appearance of the earth below which he felt desirable. So he experimented with a new picture somewhat similar in landscape design but this time leaving clear the ovoid space in which he would paint the moon. He cut a piece of glass that exact shape and then painted with thick impasto of oil on to the glass. When he was satisfied with this surface he impressed it onto the vacant space in the picture. The process of removing the glass caused the paint surfaces to be drawn upwards from the canvas thus

A Tory Wearing a Labour Mask, photograph from a collection of such with figures imposed by the artist, pen and ink on photograph on paper, 10" x 7½"

achieving that lovely texture so different from the land below. I acquired this painting 'Connemara Moon' (page 67) from him in Abbey Road in 1957 and he described the technique of its painting to me. He also told me that the picture recorded an unforgettable night in Roundstone when he and Nano Reid were walking home after a late night's drinking. 'The moon was so huge and romantic hanging over the land that even the young man in the picture was proposing marriage to the girl to whom he was making love' he told me and went on 'This never ordinarily happens there, because young men have to emigrate in order to make the money to enable them to set up a home.'

Right: 'May his goat fly away like an old paper kite', illustration from 'The Curse of Doneraile'

Below: Moon over the Bog, oil on panel, signed, 18" x 24". Sold in San Francisco 1954

Top: Richard Kingston (contemporary Irish painter), reconstructed photograph of *The Dreamer* (1956)
with Gerard Dillon photographically interposed in 1990. (See also page 37.)
Bottom: Connelly's Bar Roundstone (near Inishlackan), oil on canvas 15" x 20", signed, circa 1950. Arts Council of Northern Ireland.

9. Goodbye, Old Paint

In 1956 Victor Waddington held an exhibition in his gallery '30 Years in Dublin' which was more or less his farewell before moving to London to start his enormously successful career in Cork Street, now developed even further by his sons. A Dublin wag now refers to their several thriving galleries as Waddington Street, Cork-London. Subsequently Gerard Dillon, like many other of the artists with Waddington, entered into a new arrangement with Leo Smith of the Dawson Gallery in Dublin and for the rest of his life showed there with him. I opened his first exhibition with the Dawson Gallery and this was successful from a financial and artistic point of view. He had earlier that year exhibited four pictures in the IELA which included 'The Dreamer' (page 76) and 'Children and Chalk'. These received very warm notices and praise. They continued to emphasise his move away from landscape painting as such into work which expressed his interest in the personality and involvement of his characters, where formerly they seemed less individually observed and more part of their generic backgrounds. He had already experimented with the idea of letting the main figure become the dominant feature in his picture as in the 'Kitchen Interior' (page 67). 'The Dreamer', in particular, makes a departure in that he brings the whole figure of his subject forward so that it dominates its background. By clever use of darker tones in the foreground he creates a serenity over the furniture placing which gives stability to the composition.

At the time of this exhibition he was staying with the Dublin painter Richard Kingston, to whose work he was particularly attracted because of Kingston's very free use of paint to achieve atmosphere and his total involvement in the idea of the picture existing on its own, so to speak, independent of the subject from which it owed its original inspiration. One evening, looking at a photograph which had been reproduced in the *Irish Times* showing George Campbell seated in front of 'The Dreamer' in the Dawson Gallery, Gerard said to Richard Kingston 'I have a surrealist fantasy of putting myself into the picture in front of that young man'. This amused Richard very much and he suggested that he would take a photograph of Gerard seated in such a position. Recently when I was reminiscing with Richard he turned up the photograph from his archives, which in fact he had never used. Now some 32 years later with his enormous photographic skill he has reconstructed 'The Dreamer' with Gerard seated at the opposite end of the table (page 76) thus showing the artist inhabiting his own creation and giving existence to his fantasy, not unlike that which made the young man in the picture turn away from his book and look romantically into space.

The theme of children in the playground had interested him for its evocation of his own childhood memories and he painted a number of variations of it, perhaps also because 'the beds' on which the children play their hopscotch provokes the idea of children learning to make shapes and numbers and also because he remembered drawing with chalk in this way himself.

Shortly after that Dawson Gallery exhibition I got a letter from him which started:

Dear James, I can't wait to tell you, knowing that you'll laugh at me but no matter.

Since I got back I've been working with terrific vigour and I've gone complete abstract!!!! I'm thrilled by what I've done and so much so that I can't get to sleep for looking at them. I line them around the bed so that I can go on looking and looking and so that I can see them first thing in the morning, (if I sleep at all). I cannot describe them to you — they are almost Tachiste but not quite as they have formal qualities that most of the Tachistes lack. They have beautiful colour put on with a broad knife like 'The Dreamer' but they have passages where the paint runs down living its own life.

Now I know what Louis LeBrocquy meant when he said 'I could scrap all my past work, my other work seems so dull by comparison.' What will happen next? I don't know. Today I just finished the 16th painting and at the moment they are all around me full of active living paint. Yet they have great solemnity as well.

Now laugh at me.

On 20 February 1958, I had a further letter from him still bubbling over with excitement and full of confidence that a new world had opened up to him. In it he described his technique:

I now find abstractions are more true to nature in the long run — they are actually more natural; as if they happened by nature. They have part of the quality of the 'found object' interpreted individually by each artist. They are more like natural phenomenon, nearly as though they happened — like a surface happens to be beautiful by the cracks, swirls, lichen, seagulls droppings etc.. I've discovered a new way, an exciting way to use sand with my painting. I had it come to me out of the past, with such a difference — with years of paint knowledge, with years of cultivated taste working. Remember when you were a child — maybe you didn't do it. You found an old glass pane, spat on it and drew with the finger, spreading the spittle, then you poured fine dust or sand over the glass and the dust stuck to the spit-drawing. Well I've done that with sand, different coloured sands. (Don't tell anyone else yet about this letter nor about Gimpel and Victor W offering me exhibitions — not details anyway). I did this with paint — put on with brush, knife, pour the sand over it all, until all is sand, then tilt and let the sand run off and Lo, you have a wonderful exciting picture. It's the first time I have ever seen anything like it. I know Picasso and Braque used sand but not like this. Its completely new. George makes fun of me calling me the 'sand man'. I hope they will get me good notices when I have my show. I've done one 4 feet by 6 feet as well as about 30 or 40 others.

In the IELA of 1958, he exhibited three of his new pictures 'Goodbye Old Paint' (page 79), 'Any Old Irish Town' (page 68) and 'Not Fish nor Fowl'. Each of these, though abstract in general, nevertheless provoked known images or themes and found a ready response amongst his friends in Living Art and members of the general public who had moved into the recent international wave of abstract developments. The painter had found himself freed from the necessity to rely on nature and perspective. Instead he could follow his own impulses and seek for discovery of his inner self in the experience of responding to the pleasure of colour and texture alone, and then finding passages in which the contour excited him and he could learn a new language of which he had previously been unaware. It now became obvious what artists like Paul Klee had been experiencing 30 or forty years earlier.

In 'Goodbye Old Paint' there are clear indications of the ground and of three upright structures occupying the space. If one compares it with 'The Dreamer', the satisfactory quality finds a parallel in the late abstract work, whilst the introduction of sand into the textures gives a new interest of surface. An earlier painting, 'Whit Tuesday' (page 68), dated 1957, shows that he had been experimenting with the use of sand earlier and the title commemorates the day of the painting and the elation the artist felt in that occasion's achievement.

The painting 'Any Old Irish Town' is an extraction of the shapes of buildings freely employed to create surface textures and 'Not Fish nor Fowl' invokes shapes that intrigued him, but did not evoke any given place or thing as the title suggests.

During this period Noreen Rice and he were very involved in the idea of introducing found objects into their paintings. Noreen had discovered a dump in Brick Lane (near Petticoat Lane, in London) and the two of them would go over frequently with knapsacks on their backs to collect junk. 'We were always looking out for odd bits and pieces with which to make collages', Noreen told me and 'What would inspire Gerard seldom appealed to me and vice-versa. But we exchanged things or challenged each other with matching items. For instance I bought odd, white, kid gloves in Camden Town market. He turned out 'Glove Bird' (perfect) and mine 'Flyaway' was sold at the Lord and Taylor's New York exhibition when we showed there with other Irish artists in 1963. Gerard found two Swordfish swords in a dustbin and gave me one. We were always rushing around to see what the other had got out of these things.' Noreen also told me. 'It came to the stage that walking down the streets, our eyes were everywhere. We trained ourselves without knowing it, into fitting tops of machines (sewing machines), anything, into a picture.'

Gerard had also frequently used sacking as a base on which to paint, mounting it in pieces and joining it himself, perhaps to save the cost of buying mounted canvasses. Soon the quality of sacking appealed to him and he used sisal cord with its rough quality instead of line and developed pictures which related to the various uses of cord, including the Umbilical Cord. He exhibited 'The Honoured Cord' in the 1960 IELA and in 1962 'Sack, Sealing Wax and String' which was later retitled 'Canvas, Sealing Wax and String' perhaps because he felt it sounded grander, causing him to drop his normal love of alliteration.

Sometime before this Gerard had bought himself a second-hand sewing machine which he pressed into service to make seams in some of his sacking pictures. On one occasion he decided to make himself a suit, Noreen Rice told me, but his attempts were very amateurish. Apparently he laid down the cloth flat on the table to cut it out as if it were a drawing. Noreen had to persuade him to fold the material in two and cut it on the double in order to get both sides eventually matching. Nevertheless he told me that the presence of

the sewing machine in his flat brought back the feeling of his childhood home in Belfast.

Gerard Keenan has some excellent critical comment on this period in his serialised novel 'Farset and Gomorrah', in No 59 of *The Honest Ulsterman* for March-June 1978, pages 99 to 101. The name Francie Gent was his nom de plume for Gerard. I quote:

> On a visit to Francie Gent's around this time of turbulence Duggan and Dolly found that Francie had abandoned the figure and was painting abstracts. Or making abstracts, for the painter who had seduced Francie from the figurative was an Italian, Alberto Burri, an artist who attacked his canvas with knife, hatchet and blowlamp. Gent had always the ability to look at his paintings objectively: now he stared in bemusement at what he was producing. 'It's just like when you played babby-dishes round the entries when you were young' Gent said. 'Babby-dishes?' Duggan said. 'Yes Babby-dishes,' Dolly said sharply, angrily. 'You wouldn't know, for your Mammy never let you play around the entries.' (An echo of class differences in Farset, often evoked when Duggan and Dolly shared working-class memories.) 'I forgot he came from St Martin de Porres,' Gent said. 'There were no entries in Dublin either, but I often spent the summer holidays with an aunt in Farset and I looked forward to the seaside. The ground in the entries was like packed clay and all the old .... stoor that fell out of the bins got walked into it. Wee bits of broken cups and saucers, broken holy statues ... the Infant of Pra-

> gue's head. We picked out the pieces and washed them and then sat on the doorsteps and had you into tea. This wee bit of china was a cup, and this wee bit was your plate, and another wee bit was your teapot. If you found gold you were in heaven, the broken rim of a cup with a gold rim.' 'Oh yes. Gold' Dolly cried with pleasure. Later Dolly said, 'it was only little girls used to play house like that, bless him.'

> Mixed media was the name given to it in the galleries, but to Francie it was Babby-dishes. He had always liked making and mending — an old tweed jacket became an Aran fisherman's bawneen, one old jacket became a cloth cap, in fact. Now under the influence of Burri, he slashed his canvases and stitched them up with artistic stitching; tore holes in them and patched them with sacking or wove string across the holes like spider's webs: sought other 'random' effects by painting on board and blasting the board with his blowlamp till the painted surface bubbled like lava, burnt black or burst in splatters. He set exotic subjects in the heart of painted canvasses; an old kid glove was boiled and boiled until it was malleable, it became a bird in flight; a crocodile skin handbag, the skeleton of a swordfish from a streetmarket in Camden Town, these were rare Babby dishes, Francie had found gold in the entry. Duggan had reservations. The paintings were too beautiful....

> Francie Gent grew away from the Burri influence, and developed an individual abstract style. Over a painted abstract design he added a second abstract design using a heavy gravelly medium of sand or sand and

Above: Goodbye Old Paint, oil on canvas, 36" x 48", Exhibited IELA 1958. PC

brickdust. On a blue painted ground, as innocent, calm and unassertive as a sky by Piero della Francesco (who, indeed, had taught Gent a lot) Francie added ridges and belts of thick, gritty, reddish-brown or beige plaster like super-emery paper. ('F........ Braille paintings,' Philip Klein on a visit, commented with a laugh, and struck matches on them.) The sand paintings were successful paintings; they were confident, glowing, memorable. Gent often enjoyed them like a dis-interested spectator and amused himself looking for titles (always after the event when the painting was accomplished) that would highlight some aspect of these strange births....Istanbul, Earth Shield, Mosques. Duggan looked under the sand at the paint sub-surface, at the familiar Gent colours, at the reticent, undemonstrative, unegotistical brushwork, and regretted the times. Below the superstructure of sand were painted shapes that once had also carried information about people and the objects people live with and work with and live in and eat off. The superstructure of sand spoke only about textures, materials, interstitial space, the effect of time on surfaces and of the stuff that nature uses to make things. Sometimes, the sand shapes vaguely resembled old Celtic designs, Celtic crosses or the under-over-under-over serpentine designs of the manuscripts, and Duggan recognised that this was the end of the road down which Gauguin had led the new painters; from painting images on the walls of caves they had come to reproducing the walls of caves without the images.

All these pictures containing found objects and the like brought Gerard new patronage and in a sense lost him some of his earlier collectors who preferred his Connemara landscapes because they were more orthodox and represented the places they themselves liked whilst at the same time they were strongly marked by his individual style. Perhaps his most distinguished new patron was Sir Basil Goulding, long since come to be regarded as a courageous and innovative supporter of the arts in Ireland. He purchased 'Glove Bird' (page 81) and 'Beast Bird' referred to above as made from the unravelled crocodile lady's handbag. He also purchased 'Canvas, Sealing Wax and String' and 'One And One is One' amongst others.

In 1961, Sir Basil Goulding lent a selection from his private collection to the Municipal Gallery of Modern Art in Dublin. He entitled this 'One Man's Meat' and in the introduction he stated that the area he circumspected is Irish artists living in 1961 and painting with non-figurative intentions. His four Dillons included were those mentioned in the previous paragraph and appended to them he made these amusing remarks in his unique style:

Gerard Dillon is a constructor, and his medium is alchemy. To be brief, therefore (and thus quite a bit unfair), we need not here dilate on mood, atmosphere, nicety.

Observe, instead, how he essentially transmutes base things to precious: and agree, if you can, that he does so without mirrors, effectively, mischievous elan, compelling satisfaction; not with what is known in law as fraudulent misrepresentation.

He used to assemble only stark colour forms, and sometimes more as carpenter than joiner: now his magic may throw a timeless spell on almost anything that teases him.

Later a book was produced by Studio Vista in London entitled 'Creating in Collage' by Natalie Darbaloff and Jack Yeats in which 'The Beast Bird' and 'The Money Bird is Dead' (page 81) was first shown in 1962 at the Dawson Gallery. The bird's body was composed of a collection of old copper coins stuck on to the panel, otherwise all painted in oils, and like his other collages became a talking point for visitors to his exhibitions who found amusement in discovering the nature of the found objects in his works.

Two of his journalist friends in London, Donal Foley and Wesley Boyd, had used their influence to persuade the Irish Club in London to put on an exhibition of pictures by Dillon and George Campbell in 1955 and later both they and their wives used to visit the flat in Abbey Rd. Wesley Boyd remembers Gerard boiling leather gloves on his stove to get the dye out of them. He also recalls that Gerard came across a photographic plate of one of his paintings 'The Falls Road on a Saturday Night' (page 81) and he used this to print it on paper in sepia tones and then took the print and added to it a print of his self portrait and inscribed the names of their children over the shop fronts: thus making a most personal present for both the Boyd and the Foley families. He also made one of these for this writer's family and inscribed it with the names of his daughter Catherine and son Peter during a visit to Dublin at the time. The painting 'The Falls Road on a Saturday Night' commemorated home during his childhood for Gerard but it also gave a measure of gaiety and colour by the use of street lights and shopfronts to the Falls Road scene and Lower Clonard Street where Gerard lived, which contrasts with his earlier paintings of the scene always marked by their air of comparative poverty and greyness. This belonged to Donal Foley

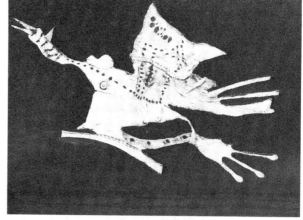

Right: Glove Bird, oil and kidd leather on panel, 14½" x 19¼".
Exhibited IELA 1961. PC

Below: Gerard holding *The Money Bird is Dead,* oil and coins on
board, 9" x 13". Exhibited in the Dawson Gallery, Dublin, 1962

Bottom: Etching after *The Falls Road on a Saturday Night* with
self portrait interposed and titles imposed on shop fronts,
etching on paper, 5"x9". (See page 22.)

and when he died he left the picture to Douglas Gageby, then editor of the *Irish Times* and a Belfast man himself. The painting was later reproduced in that paper to illustrate an article on the Mouth of The Farset River in Belfast and the course it takes through the city. The prevalence of Northern Ireland journalists in the Dublin newspaper world has always been notable and Dillon was a favourite visitor to their pub-haunts in Fleet Street during his Dublin visits.

Gerard had always tended to make his own prints with linocuts, woodcuts or by monotype and many of his friends still treasure the Christmas cards they received from him over the years. On page 83 is a small selection from my own collection. Each year he made a standard Christmas scene but he frequently added to it a personal sketch or colours appropriate to the friend to whom he was sending it.

The variety of styles and innovations which he had introduced in to his paintings in the middle fifties greatly enhanced his standing on the international scene. This was made apparent by his inclusion as a British artist in an announcement in the British press which read 'Twenty three painters and twelve sculptors have been chosen to represent Great Britain in the 1958 Carnegie Prize exhibition to be held in the Carnegie Institute in Pittsburgh from December 5th to February 8th 1959.' The list is then given which includes almost every distinguished, living, British artist of the time including Bacon, Hitchens, Nicholson, Scott, Spencer, Sutherland, Epstein, Hepworth, Moore and Paolozzi and of course in the midst of all that notoriety, Gerard Dillon. This was probably the first and only time that Gerard did not protest at having himself described as British. It also gave him a sense of confidence in his own progression as a painter who could now regard himself as accepted in Britain and not feel regarded as merely 'interesting Irish'. At this exhibition his 'Ascelt Group' was purchased by the Carnegie Trust.

In 1958 he had been selected with several other artists to represent Ireland at the International prize exhibition in the Solomon Guggenheim Gallery in New York. One of his sand pictures 'Sea Beast Basking' was included. Again in 1962, he was selected at a similar exhibition in New York and this time he was represented by the abstract 'Masquerade' (page 85). Then in 1962 for the Marzotto International exhibition in Rome his 'The Side of The Hill' (page 85) was selected. He was again included

in the Marzotto International in Rome in 1963 and his painting 'In the Swirl of The Blue Wind' received an award.

By this time he must have felt aware that he had emerged from the shadows and was known. Shortly afterwards he received a call asking him to bring some pictures to be shown to film stars Richard Burton and Elizabeth Taylor at their London Hotel. He duly hired a taxi and brought a number of paintings and carried them up to their rooms. He waited for over an hour, during which period a maid would emerge from time to time stating that they would be with him in a minute or two. Eventually the maid announced that they could not see him now as they were late for an appointment. He was absolutely furious and left in a rage. Later they sent him a cheque for £20 to cover the time and trouble caused. He tore up the cheque and posted the pieces back to them without comment. However in March 1965 they visited the Dawson Gallery where they purchased one of his paintings.

In 1952 he had been employed by Córas Tráchtála (The Irish Export Board) in Dublin to assist in a promotion of goods in Macy's Store in New York which took place during the St. Patrick's Day celebrations and also contributed a panel for it. In October 1963 he participated in a promotion in Lord and Taylor's in New York. There were twenty four window displays and the store was devoted to the promotion of Irish made goods of all kinds. A party of 137 representatives of industrial designers, artists and officials was flown out for this occasion and they included Norah McGuinness, Anne Yeats and Gerard Dillon, all three members of the IELA committee. At the same time the Irish Arts Council had organised an exhibition in the 'New School for Social Research' of Irish artists' work and Gerard had six of his recent pictures included.

As John F. Kennedy was then President of the U.S.A., he invited the party to travel to a reception in the White House in Washington. At this time Gerard had left New York to visit relations in Michigan and he subsequently travelled by Greyhound Bus to Washington for the occasion. Anne Yeats remembers him arriving late to the hotel after a long and tiring journey and wearily making his way up to bed. When he got to his room he found it already occupied by a glamorous, blonde girl. In due course he got himself more suitably allocated and with the rest of the party was received next day by President Kennedy.

Most unexpected objects continued to figure

in his works. In 1962 he showed a sculpture entitled 'King and Queen' at the IELA, which arose from an amusing incident. His friend Joseph Quilty told me that one of his pupils, the wife of a successful business man, knocked on his door in the early hours of one morning. When he opened it there stood his friend and good patron, Mrs B., with a large black eye. 'God, what are you doing at this hour of the night' he said. 'You'll have to let me in and give me a bed,' she replied. Gerard didn't like the idea of having a woman in the house, but when she explained the circumstances, he let her stay. Apparently she had been out all day visiting her artistic friends. When she arrived home her husband was furious and he said to her 'Where's your Amber necklace?' She had lost it. He struck her in the face with his fist and she left him and didn't want to go back until the next morning when he had left for work. During the course of getting undressed in Gerard's spare bedroom, a couple of the Amber beads fell on the floor. 'Ah,' she said to Gerard the next morning, 'you might as well have them.'

When Mrs B. had left, Gerard went down to his garden where he had two old spade handles. He brought them in, cleaned them up, mounted them on a base and inserted the Amber beads on the little knobs on either side of the spade handles. He told Joseph that he christened them 'Mr and Mrs Spade Handle.' Later he entitled them 'King and Queen' (no doubt enjoying the thought that they were the King and Queen of his spades.) They were acquired by Sir Basil Goulding who was even more enamoured by this association.

A selection of Christmas cards.

10. Last Days in Abbey Road

In October 1962, I was asked to comment on a painting of Gerard's 'The Crowning with Thorns' (page 86) reproduced in the excellent religious magazine *Doctrine and Life* published in Dublin by the Dominican Fathers and from which I quote:

> Gerard Dillon's 'Crowning with Thorns' has the kind of realism which is almost unbearable to contemplate. It brings one face to face with the sheer physical suffering, through the prominence of the plait of large spines, impossible to imagine until one encounters a thorn when clamouring through a hawthorn or bramble hedge. Then the mind realises in miniature form what a hundred such incisions must feel like in the tender surface of the cranium. No matter what suffering a human being endures, however, he has it. Every man knows that even if the particular perpetrator of his torments has no justification, somewhere in his own life there is a crime to be redressed. The artist who depicts Christ's sufferings must endeavour to convey the fact that they were totally unjust. Perfect love has been violated. Those perfectly loved have retaliated with indecent, indecorous and brutal assault. No artist has succeeded in this task nor will it ever be done.
>
> The reproduction of this picture perhaps accentuates unduly the pathetic, almost quivering sense of pain. Yet the hard, black eyes are accusing. And beauty of feature has been preserved. In the original, colour helps to underline the subject, purples and greens are interwoven and what seems smooth here is there much rougher and more varied in texture. In spite of the great variety of tones apparent, the transference to black and white has removed the evidences of technique employed by the artist.
>
> Gerard Dillon has long been regarded as one of the most inveterate experimenters with the various materials that can be introduced into oil painting. This picture, however, is part collage, part monotype and part gouache. The sharp edge will indicate to a keen eye the imprint of a plate. In this case the plate was a sheet of glass which had picked up the painted image from another paper. This method produces the lovely texture visible in the face. The eyes, the nostrils, several of the thorns and other marks are composed of pieces of paper cut out and stuck onto the surface (collage). Finally, of course, the artist uses the brush directly to complete the desired effects. Were it not for the combination of effects thus achieved the picture would have a very different aspect. He who asks why the painter does not use brush and pigment alone to simulate the appearance here fails to appreciate the fact that in this kind of art the creator does not himself know what his picture will look like until it is finished. He starts off in search of a certain effect. On the way he encounters unexpected opportunities of which he avails. When he decides to stop he may have made many new discoveries.
>
> The patches of shadow on the face, the distortions of the mouth, the trickles of blood accord with what the artist imagines when he contemplates the suffering of Our Lord. But his statement of them is not so much calculated as inspired by the moment of excitement which is part of the inspiration of the artist. In former times the painter tended to be more guided by physical appearances. In our time psychic experience is the most potent factor. Thus the artist uses new and hitherto unknown means to reach behind the outer image so that the inner meaning of the subject may be enlarged upon.

The brutality of Christ's scourging and crucifixion always horrified Dillon and he said several times that he could not bring himself to treat of that subject although he had painted it directly from Celtic stone carvings many times. In the case of the stone carvings he was mainly concerned to capture the feeling and atmosphere of that ancient world and he saw the forms as symbols rather than as recreations of feeling as in the case of this picture. However his sensibilities did not preclude him from the subject of Veronica's Veil which he had made for his longtime friend Madge Connolly. The idea of the image within the Veil with which Veronica wiped the face of Jesus was one which he attempted several times, and this Crowning with Thorns is an evolution of the earlier one, greatly elaborated by the use of collage strips and his monotype techniques to heighten the contrast between flesh tones and the actual thorns. When he considered the brutality of which man was capable by nailing hands and feet to a wooden cross, Gerard's whole being revolted. Accidents, cruelty to animals and the continued persecution of minorities, indeed every form of cruelty caused him anguish and made him turn away in horror and seek the solace of his own creative work. He went so far at times as to get cross with his friends and pupils who did not show proper application to their work and many of them recall how he railed at them for their ambitions and desires for material possessions. On one occasion when a friend had no food left in her flat, he went to her refuse bin and

Above: *Masked Female Artist and Black Girl with Bird,* oil on panel, 13"x16", signed, circa 1961. PC. This picture may represent Noreen Rice.

Left: *The Crowning with Thorns,* media and monotype on paper, 20"x12", 1962. Dominican Order Dublin

Previous page top: *Masquerade,* oil and sand on panel, 36"x46", signed. Exhibited Dawson Gallery 1959. Guggenheim New York International Award 1960. Taylor Galleries Dublin.

Previous page bottom: *The Side of a Hill,* oil and sand on board, 30"x40", signed. Marzotto European Community 1962 Painting Award. Taylor Galleries Dublin.

Facing page top: *Entertaining Friends,* oil on canvas, 30"x25", signed. Exhibited Dawson Gallery 1968. Institute of Public Administration, Dublin

Facing page bottom: *The Brothers,* oil on canvas, 48"x36". Exhibited Dawson Gallery 1968. Taylor Galleries Dublin

Page 88: *Wandering Through Life,* oil and string on canvas, 44"x30". Exhibited IELA 1966. Taylor Galleries Dublin

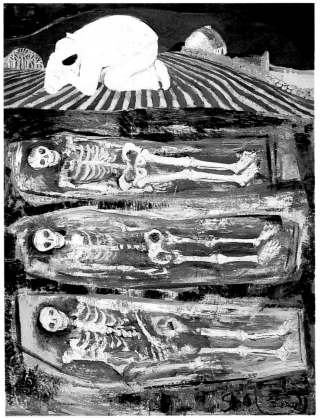

finding there a loaf of bread and some cheese, thrown out because they were mildewed, he took them out and cutting away the mildewed exteriors he ate them, saying 'What a waste throwing out good food. My dear, if I were you, I'd buy paint with the money saved.'

To some extent he used his dedication to his art as a replacement for the religion he had relinquished as a teenager and regarded the discipline it imposed on him as a substitute for the presence of a mother, or some such intimate associate involved in his life.

In 1963, twenty years after its first showing, the IELA held its finest and most forward-looking exhibition. Thanks to James Johnston Sweeney, then Irish-American Director of the Museum of Fine Arts in Houston, Texas, 12 really outstanding modern American paintings were loaned, all representing the new wave of abstract art. These artists were James Brooks, Stuart Davis, DeKooning, Gottlieb, Sam Francis, Johns, Marca Relli, Motherwell, O'Keeffe, Rauschenberg, Rothko and Tobey and they created a new standard by which the artists of Ireland might be judged. Dillon's pictures fitted harmoniously into this background. Two of them had already been seen in New York, 'Sea Beast Basking' and 'Bagdad', and together with 'Expanding Form' represented his most recent style of confecting surfaces which did not depend on direct figurative sources.

On his return to London, he was extremely disturbed to learn that Molly had been informed by London Borough Council that the Abbey Road houses were being compulsorily bought and she had been given notice to quit. They had of course to set about getting new quarters and Gerard was eventually allotted a two room flat in 3 Greville Road, NW6. Life had been ideal for him in the Abbey Road basement, especially since Hugh Heanon had left and he could occupy it all. As well as the three principal rooms, he had a storage closet and a fine shed fitted with beds in the garden where close friends could put up for a spell in fine weather. His accumulation of art equipment, including a ton of fine sand thrown in a corner of the garden, and all his pictures and books would never again be housed so conveniently.

At first they only offered him a single room but because his home had been compulsorily acquired and because he was a painter living from his work 'they begrudgingly gave me two rooms, saying that it was only until a one-room flatlet was available. They said I'd have to rent a studio separately. It wasn't their concern that someone should run a business in his home. They didn't allow it in fact. That's how they looked on painting — a business' he told me, 'And they regretted that they had to let me have a two-room flat because one-room flatlets were short at the time. They tried to make me share it with some strange man they needed to house. Anyway you can understand why I didn't feel at home in this place, tho' it's OK. It's just the Hall flat in an ordinary house — front room and back room, off that a WC and bathroom combined, and a very small kitchen off the hall. I built a canopy over the put-u-up (bed) down from the ceiling and hand-painted curtains to cover the pictures, stored inside.'

He also wrote 'The neighbours in the house feel a certain resentment that I got a flat. I overheard the kids from next door talking about me "It's a shame that a single man should get a flat when one room would do him." This is the general thinking of council tenants — what these couples never stop doing is filling the place with one kid after another so all local Governments should be looking after their welfare and nobody else's. So I'm sure I'm looked on as an oddity and allowed to slip in and out, ignored almost. That suits me in many ways, but still its not nice to know that you are resented.' He finally added 'In the small front hall you get groups chattering. When this happens and I'm not about to go out — I have to wait until they go away, I can't bear pushing through them. I feel too shy for this. Or the women might be gossiping at the garden gate and I wait and wait — I feel it's better to keep out of sight — for out of sight is out of mind.'

A great deal of all the over-sensibility about this new flat and its surroundings was caused in the first instance because the lady occupying the basement flat complained, Joe Quilty told me. 'Gerard was in the habit of working late at night and even until 3 or 4 in the morning. When he went to his new flat he had to buy some builder's sand to use in his paintings. But it wasn't clean. So he decided to filter it and he bought a little sieve — a housekeeper's sieve for filtering flour. And he spread a newspaper on the floor at 3 AM and he shook the sand through the sieve onto the paper. The following morning the lady from below came to him and said "Mr Dillon, I can't understand what's happening in the house. I couldn't sleep a wink last night." "I am sorry to hear that," he replied, "what seems to be the matter?" "I keep waking up," she said, "and all I can hear is this Tch, Tch, Tch, Tch." She could hear the sand falling on the paper in the silence of the night.'

Eventually the occupant of the basement flat left and was replaced by a couple who worked by day, so he confined his activities to their absences, but was extremely unhappy once they were present in the house lest he might disturb them. Several of his friends felt that the move to Greville Road and the disruption of his former comparatively peaceful existence was a contributory cause to an illness which was to follow.

There had, in fact, been some previous indications of Gerard having heart pains. Wesley Boyd recalls that just before he returned to Ireland in 1961 Gerard got ill and he and his wife felt apprehensive that the cause might be his heart. Then in December 1962, his brother Joe died. Of all the family Joe was the one to whom he was most attached. They were two of a kind. Joe the musician, Gerard the painter — both confirmed bachelors whose lives were led in the pursuit of the art which attracted them. Some time later Gerard gave Madge Connolly a painting 'And The Time Passes.' It showed two masked pierrots, one dressed all in white moving out of the picture, the other in striped and coloured costume, his hand holding the hand of the departing pierrot and his other hand held up in the farewell gesture, an empty chair nearby as a symbol of the departed. They are placed on the shore with the sea and the sky behind. One suspects that this is a summing up of their days together and now Joe's departure from life. The title suggests the fact of Gerard's first encountering Madge when he came to London to join Joe and Pino in 1934, some 28 years previously.

Gerard commenced to paint pictures of pierrots with masks from this time forward and for the remaining years of his life. On one occasion when Tom McCreanor remarked that there was a feeling of sadness in his early Pierrot pictures, Gerard replied, 'I think it's nature's way of letting you know that you are on the way out.' Gerard had painted clowns as subjects earlier but these were related to his interest in circus life as part of drama and also because of the frequency with which artists used clowns as symbols of the entertainer behind whose make-up might lie a broken heart.

Throughout the past three centuries the clown, pierrot or harlequin has been frequently used by painters such as Watteau, Tiepolo, Goya and so on to represent the tragedies and follies of mankind when it has not been politic for the artist to select recognisable figures from life for his satires. One of the most famous recent instances was when Picasso's mistress, Eva Gouel, died of tuberculosis in 1915 — thus 'his state of mind is evident in the ominous black background and sinister smile of the harlequin he painted that autumn.' (Theodore Reff in 'The Sketchbooks of Picasso', Thames and Hudson, 1986.)

The many such examples in the history of painting no doubt inspired Dillon, but one assumes that it was Picasso's example which most of all encouraged him to project himself personally into his pictures by the use of the masked pierrot. Prior to Joe's death and his involvement in abstract painting he had seemed to exult in the costume pictures of Connemara since they represented the ideal Ireland of his dreams. Now with the device of pierrot figures, elegantly draped (perhaps the artistic parallel in his mind of the robed priests performing church ceremonies), he was able to be a participant in the various figure studies he devised. The most common of these showed the pierrot as artist involved with a second figure as muse or inspiration. On one occasion, wishing to paint his friend, Noreen Rice as the artist, holding her palette and brushes, he dispensed with the pierrot costume but showed her naked and standing beside her easel on which is painted her muse as a black girl, holding a songbird on her fingertips (page 86). This picture is somewhat abstracted and makes no attempt to represent his subject from life, but rather to reflect the woman artist in his intimate circle of friends.

In the end pages of another artist's catalogue around this time, he made a series of quick pen sketches with his usual fine line, hitting the exact parts of the paper to describe the kneeling pierrot and dog (Joe was invariably accompanied by his dog) above the ground, underneath which is placed in the left sketch two coffins and in the right sketch a single coffin (page 92). In the first sketch, the second coffin apparently housing a skeleton may represent a former burial. Moving across to the second sketch, the pierrot is much better drawn and the indication of a mound of earth beneath the pierrot's knees more clear. The dog in the second sketch has been given a mourning expression. This drawing I take to represent himself praying over his brother Joe's grave, for it anticipates his apprehension of his own death as well as the fact that in August 1964 his brother Patrick died, and in December 1966, his brother John died, each as a result of heart defects. But already in his show in the

2) + these new paintings of mine have colours that Matisse would have liked.

Well James I wish you all the best

Yours Gerard

P.S. There are notes of colour on Back of snaps. I also did a big one of 3 skeletons in a Grave I think it's the best in the show — tho' I wouldn't say this, roughly like this — it's all red browns, and above ground is blue + yellowish stripes Pierrot in white. dark mountain + sky. I think it's an important pic in my life of painting. Called "The Brothers".

The whole show is cheerful in colour has a humour with underlying sadness about it — is poetic (I think) Is very subconscious indeed — they all came from the side of me that's over there!

Well James I'll get this off again thank you.

Gerard

Dawson Gallery in 1965 he exhibited 'The Brothers' (page 92). A number of sad pictures were to follow concerned not just with the deaths of three of his brothers over a five-year period but also because he felt that he, himself had not long to live and in fact he began to forecast that he would not pass his 55th year.

In the IELA of 1965, he showed four related paintings. One of these, 'Pierrot and Picture' shows the pierrot seated on the ground with his left hand over his eyes as if to suggest that the burden of grief was great. The landscape behind is a linear one with farm outhouses and machinery. He also exhibited two somewhat similar subjects, 'Mask and Canvas' and 'Masked Figure and Nude', and another work 'Hypnotic Mask' which was a painted relief put together with collage to give the impression of the clown-mask penetrated by light to reveal only squares for your eyes and a triangle for

Above: Last page of letter from Dillon to James White showing *Clown Listening to the Earth*

nose — as if to say 'if you penetrate the mask you will not find a human.'

The complexity of his thinking at this time is apparent in these images based on the concept of the impersonal pierrot substituted for himself. He now represented his figures with a more classical clear line and almost all his works of the period have a cool, colour tonality and are in contrast to the expressionist, abstract works which preceded them and in which line and contour are somewhat interpenetrated. Strangely enough in the exhibitions in the Dawson Gallery of 1965 and the RHA of 1965 and of 1966, all of these clown or pierrot pictures were given clown titles. There were some 20 paintings with clown titles in the Dawson Gallery exhibition of 1965 and it is difficult to estimate if he was indifferent to the name or if he felt that they represented similar themes. In later years he avoided either word and found his titles from the spirit or subject which moved him.

In the 1966 Dawson Gallery exhibition he showed the poignant 'Three Brothers' (page 87) which was the large painting based on the drawings already referred to. Somewhat later he again returned to the subject and wrote me in February 1967 about an introduction which I was to write for his show in the Mercury Gallery, London, that year. He referred to his newer paintings as 'pierrots in poetic fantasies.' I reproduce page 2 of this letter (page 91) as it contains a hasty sketch of 'The Brothers' (page 92) which he exhibited in the 1967 IELA. In his postscript to the letter he wrote 'I also did a big one of three skeletons in a grave. I think it is the best in the show — tho' I shouldn't say this, roughly like this — its all red browns and above ground is blue and yellowish stripes, pierrot in white, dark mountains and sky. I think it is an important pic. in my life of painting. Called 'The Brothers'. The whole show is cheerful in colour, has a humour with underlying sadness about it — is poetic (I think). Is very subconscious, indeed they all come from the side of me that's "over there".'

The 1966 'Three Brothers' was somewhat more bizarre, since it showed the three skeletons below ground and only a cross and wreaths above. Another bizarre picture in the

Above: Drawings for *The Brothers*, from a sketch book, pen on paper, 8" x 10"

Mercury Gallery exhibition was called 'Entertaining Friends' (page 87) and here he shows three masked clowns in costume, heavily draped with leaves and foliage seated before a table on which is placed 4 cups and saucers, etc.. The host clown is on the right and holds a rose in his hand. The implication that he saw himself entertaining these three ghostly apparitions of his brothers seems very likely.

Although the change in his style following his three brother's deaths brought about an end to his abstract period, he continued to play around with ready-made objects. From his store of previously used wood and lino blocks from which he had made prints, in most cases for Christmas cards over the years, he made a gouache of a pierrot standing beside his easel on which has been printed a series of these prints assembled together and painted over, which he called 'Dark Pierrot with Dark Canvas.' He declared his use of these prints in the picture 'Yellow Panel of Christmases Past' exhibited in the Northern Ireland Arts Council exhibition of 1966. There were, however, a number of most poetic pierrot and clown paintings exhibited in the period of his residence in Greville Road which expressed his urge to release himself as artist into the world of dreams, such as 'Wandering through Life' (page 88) in which he returned once again to the use of cord, perhaps to symbolise the idea of the tape-roll of memory on which is recorded all those happenings of the past which come flooding into the mind when the eyes are closed. 'Once upon a Wavelength' (page 107) combines the idea of the desert island nude being rescued by the pierrot, whilst the clouds above contain the shapes of floating nudes. Occasionally one dreams of being released from one's contact with earth and free to float above the land with the delightful capacity to zoom up and down at will. Strangely this dream is experienced from time to time by people in many parts of the world, according to records made.

Sometime in 1967 Gerard had joined a life class at the Sarah Siddons school in Paddington Institute in London. Drawings and paintings of nudes became frequent in his work and his gift in this direction is recorded in many such sketches and no doubt inspired many of the paintings of the period such as 'Connemara Dream' with the figure of the nude, legs drawn up in a chair in such a pose as one might expect in a life class.

During the late summer of 1967 he confided to his friend Dr Maura McQuaid that he was having heart pains. She arranged to have him enter the Royal Homeopathic Hospital in Queensway for a check-up. He wrote from there to his nephew Gerard that he had had a coronary and had been in for four weeks. He added 'I feel like I've walked the path of life on to the lane that leads to the tomb. There's no doubt about that. Looking around me here I can see that death has put his hand on each one of us.'

He went to stay with his sister Molly in Lithos Road in Hampstead to recuperate. When he eventually got back to his flat in Greville Road and saw all his paintings again, he cried with joy, Molly informed me in a letter. It was then that she told me that it was the discomforts of that flat and of the pressures of his neighbours which were the cause of this illness and the ultimate cause of his death.

All his friends rallied round after his return to Greville Road and his nephew Gerard came to stay for a period and helped him to stretch canvases for painting. In an enthusiastic letter to his nephew he described how busy he was again painting. He was using cut-out shapes which had taken human forms as in the clouds of 'Magic in The Sky' (page 105). In that letter of April 1968 he wrote:

It's great fun trying to get the optical illusion of now one minute the shape is receding and now coming forward. It's the difficulty that makes it worth while attempting — the result is decorative primarily, I suppose with an undercurrent for surrealism. The cut-out shapes have taken human forms [and then he interposes the drawing].' He goes on, 'This is the big one and its green on a blue background and it succeeds in this optical way which is very fascinating. I've got a good name for it too. The actual picture makes the little white pierrot look small and lost in the bigness of the world, so I've the right and good name for it which has a touch of humour in it as well 'Heavens Above'! Anyway it's great and these four I'm just working on are opening another door, more exploration, as it were, and that is always a delight. Makes me feel with it again somehow.

In the event, when he showed it in the IELA in 1968, he dropped the name 'Heavens Above' and called it 'Cut out, Drop out' (page 106). In the catalogue (1986) of the Allied Irish Banks Collection in which it is reproduced, that shrewd art historian, Frances Ruane, added this comment:

'Cut out, Drop out' is a late work of the painter Gerard Dillon (1916-1971). The pierrot/artist sits contemplating his life, or perhaps more specifically, the fleeting nature of his existence. Dillon had an illness from which three of his brothers died, so he was eventually preoccupied with death, a theme which recurs in several mature works. In 'Cut out, Drop out' the pierrot/artist observes cut-out visions of himself floating overhead, ghostly and without physical substance. He fails to notice the sturdy young plant growing beside him which is apparently a suggestion of continuity and regeneration. Looking at the lonely figure, we briefly share his isolation as he sits detached from the rest of the world.

He had already had a successful show in the Dawson Gallery in June 1968 and although it included 'The Brothers' the general atmosphere was bright and colourful. 'In the Blue Hills' (page 94), for instance, was a delightful floating image of the pierrot/artist contacting a young girl in a swirl of dreams. Like most artists Dillon was well able to escape into such romantic retreats from the darker effects of his bodily complaints. He also introduced some of his kite pictures into the exhibition and one of these, 'The Frightened Kite', expressed his ability to find release from the practicalities of domestic realism and in general from coping with an existence no longer as manageable and easy to handle. To some extent he was cut off from ease of travel and most of all from contact with his beloved Western Ireland. In consequence during the remaining years of his life, his subjects were to be confined to works of his imagination in which the landscape and other backgrounds would be extracted from

the great store of memory which he had acquired in nearly forty years, not to mention the large collection of sketches and watercolours also preserved.

Top: Shy Sweetheart, collage on board, 26" x 18". Exhibited Dawson Gallery, Dublin, 1969. PC

Left: In the Blue Hills, oil on canvas, 34" x 42", signed. Exhibited Dawson Gallery, 1968. PC

11. The Last of London

During early summer of 1968, Gerard was visited in Greville Road and informed that he was once again going to be re-housed. This worried him greatly because of the difficulties he had had in making the present flat suitable as a studio and to accommodate all his books and pictures. He wrote to his nephew, Gerard 'I've been burning and burning, sorting out everything, burned loads of my early drawings and water colours. Keeping only the pick or the ones that might hold an idea for a picture. There's no use in being held down by things that make bulk and weight.'

In fact he had actually signed for a new flat and applied to have his telephone transferred before he went over to Dublin for his Dawson Gallery exhibition. Whilst there, George Campbell persuaded him and Arthur Armstrong to take a house jointly in Dublin. The thought had not occurred to Gerard before but once the idea was mooted he agreed. George and Madge lived in Ranelagh, and Gerard frequently stayed with them. They saw a house for sale nearby, No 28 Chelmsford Road, and suggested that they should buy it. This all happened very quickly and Gerard had to return to London and cancel his previous arrangements. He wrote to a friend explaining why he had to leave London:

> I had been messed about over hanging space and I would love a house with a garden, which this one in Dublin has — none in the front but a long narrow one at the back opening onto a mews; all trees, with six rooms and when you paint all the time the work gathers up until you are swamped under. Arthur, too, is a prolific worker and he is in the same position and he's had these last few years, messed about from one furnished bedsitter to the next and it will be a great mental relief to him too. He's a quiet fellow with no notion of marrying, I've known and shared long spells with him over the years, so know what he's like to live with.

Once his mind was made up, Gerard acted fast. He made arrangements with the local authority and started once again the process of moving his possessions. In the autumn the packers came. In his own words 'They sent a lovely container and spent hours packing everything well and safely'. Unfortunately these were all transferred into a large container for shipping and almost everything got wet and damaged in this process. Many of his books were ruined beyond repair but only a few of his pictures. However he and Arthur worked hard and long during coming months and they were almost established in comfort by Christmas. In a letter to his nephew he described it graphically:

> I haven't been able to lift my head since I arrived with work of all sorts — but I never felt better. I think not living alone is a great help. All the responsibilities aren't on your own shoulders alone. We have our separate rooms — small bed-sitters as it were — with a communal studio, dining room and visitors parlour (if we need it and when we get it finished.) We share meals — he or I cooking as the mood takes us. Arthur usually lights the fire, and makes the breakfast and I make the evening meal, but it isn't rigid in any way. What we've done — dug up a whole half grown hedge from the Campbells and replanted it in our back garden. Tarred a long working kitchen roof — built a dresser in there too and a work bench. Painted the stairs and staircase and hall, done up my room, papered and built bookcase, painted his room and built a sort of false floor in one corner for books, gramophone etc.. Painted the dining room, whitewashed the yard, painted the front parlour. Got the slates seen to all over the house. Built racks in the studio to hold pictures — got the bedroom shipshape — return room still has to have racks built for storing pictures. The hall floor has to be lifted and old bad joists lifted and renewed in places. Its a fulltime job but we are beginning to get things sort of straight and now each in his room is at last feeling at home. But it will be a while before we can get all in order.

Further on he wrote 'I wish it had been spring when we moved in instead of winter. Its always more pleasant doing jobs when its bright and getting brighter. Anyway, we've done a lot to the garden, set a lot and if all goes well it will be a great place to be out working in when the Spring does come.'

In spite of this report of avid house activity, he still found time to do some experimenting with design and he was also commissioned in a couple of comparatively new activities. RTE, the Irish television company requested him to design their Christmas card for 1968 (page 97). For this he combined the Connemara landscape with the general idea of early stonecarvings as a background to one of his characteristic Holy Family groups. In painting this group he followed the naive style of Gauguin (based on the wayside Crucifixion groups of Brittany) which he had used all over the years for his private Christmas cards. For him it reflected the sentimental Christmassy style which he felt appropriate for its general use in Ireland, especially the image of the Christ Child radiating from a bed of straw in the manner of the plaster figures commonly used in domestic cribs. He made a pattern out of the birds, dog and cat to close off the foreground and to pick up the flow of the arms of the Cross above. On close analysis the naivety of the card seems overdone. But when viewed in the context of an array of cards on a shelf, its boldness of design and colour must surely have enabled it to stand out prominently.

The second unexpected commission came from the Abbey Theatre who were planning a new production of the O'Casey play 'Juno and The Paycock'. They asked the three Belfast artists Armstrong, Campbell and Dillon to design the settings and costumes for it. Earlier in 1967, these three artists had been invited to design posters for the newly built Abbey Theatre, which had previously been destroyed by fire. Gerard's commission was for the O'Casey play 'Red Roses for Me' (page 98). His poster was based on street flower-sellers on the left and two gangers on the right, both groups typifying Dublin characters of the time and heavily outlined in black and touched with green and grey. Then with his recent graceful, romantic line, he shows two boys soar above on the right, one holding red roses aloft and two similarly robed girls above the left group, reaching for the flowers. His natural graphic skill is demonstrated in the arms of these four balletic, young people whose movement draws all attention to the Red Roses of the play, which opened in August, 1967.

During the period of moving in to Chelmsford Road, the three friends were at work on the costumes and sets for 'Juno and The Paycock' (first performed in The Abbey Theatre in March 1924). The programme credits the design to A.D.C. 1969, and explains in a note:

Arthur Armstrong, Gerard Dillon and George Campbell are the three artists whose initials make up the A.D.C. 1969 credit for the design of 'Juno and The Paycock.' This is not their first connection with the Abbey Theatre, as they designed the first three posters for the new Abbey. The posters sprang from their belief that artists should be closely involved with all artistic efforts in the country.

The three artists have many things in common, a love of Spain, connections with Belfast, close friendship over many years, and a belief that artists should not be isolated in their work. All this has helped in producing a unified design.

One disadvantage which Gerard now discovered about Dublin was that unlike his life in London he found difficulty in escaping to the privacy of his own home. In a letter to a friend he wrote:

Sometimes I ask myself, am I happy by the move to Dublin? Most times I have to answer 'yes'. But very often its 'no'. I really don't know. It has helped me moneywise, but that's all to go to pay my debts, house, etc..... I spend more as my friends around me live a more extravagant standard of life. My life in London was more simple, frugal even. Tho' I never did without the necessities. Coming here has affected my working power and I'm doing some lovely work and wonder would it be so lovely if I was back in London.

In a letter to a painter friend in London he refers to these first months in Dublin thus:

I still don't know that I'm living in Dublin. Why? Because I have been so busy getting the place to look like home. George says when he looks 'Bringing Kilburn over here.' Now its nearly like home. I have earned some money since I got here, I did the Christmas card for T.V. for which they paid me well. When I think of the years I did hand-done Christmas cards for 1/- and 1/6 P. and each one different — God its changed times. I got Gns80 for this one. I felt ashamed in a way, felt like Dick Turpin! Robbing the rich to give to the poor me. I got Gns21 from the Abbey Theatre for the sale of the poster and this they say will go on. Gns20 from the National Gallery for painting for the kids — that was an experiment that I dreaded but now its over I know I had nothing to fear. It was so easy. The morning session 11 a.m. to 12 a.m. I had about 500 from 12 to 18 years old. Then from 3 to 4 p.m. I had 900 from 7 to 12. They were the best. They were lovely children from all classes — good schools to back street kids. They loved it so it made me love it — lovely to see the mums waiting patiently down the stairs — no adults were allowed in. I talked into a 'mike' around my neck so hadn't the bother of shouting to be heard. It wasn't really what I thought. I got a big sheet 5ft by 4ft and did what design I'd already done of the panels from the old Celtic crosses — which naturally held great interest for them and as each panel was colourful and with Adam and Eve, Cain killing Abel and the wiseman and Christ and birds, dogs and fish — I worked like mad, a bit here and a bit there not completing any one panel — but bringing them along bit by bit. What I didn't know beforehand was that they all had their jamjars full of water and their book and any time I looked around to say 'Are you alright', all heads would pop up to shout 'Ye....essss.' All you could hear was the tinkling of the camelhair brushes on the jars like goat bells. When it was all over they

mobbed me with questions, wanting my name on their bits of paper — I said 'Isn't it funny I can't write, although I can paint — Isn't that odd?' One said 'Then who signs your pictures for you?' 'My Mother' I replied but in two seconds I signed a few and said my wrist was tired as surely they'd watched me for the last hour jumping about from table to easel like an eijit. So they let me off. The older ones I found more difficult as I worked in oils and they too were doing their copies — but James White told me I was to talk while I worked — this after five minutes I found foolish — did you ever talk and never get an answer — I said this 'Its like talking to a stone wall talking to you lot.' That got a laugh. When I finished what I'd done — I turned to talk and explain that this would really be only an under painting for the time wouldn't allow for anything else. Also that you must have courage after you got this far. When they said they'd liked what I had done, I quietly got a big brush and swiped it all off at great speed and they clapped and clapped. Maybe they were glad to see it wiped out, you couldn't really tell, if it was for that or my cheek to blot it out. Then I showed them how the messed about

board might feed their imaginations and how you might see something you hadn't thought about. So I looked and then painted something that the paint suggested to me — they loved this. I rubbed this out at speed ending with a dull greenish-blue mess and with a rag I dashed three cleaner swipes like Hartung in shape. Later a boy brought up a board with this mess and the 3 cleaner swipes (copied) for me to see. Down in the entrance hall as I waited for a taxi, after the younger lot, a little fair palefaced boy about 7 with a sturdy dark rosy-faced sister — said 'Are you coming again next year? Then he said 'You're very good-looking, 'Oh, thank you,' I replied 'And you are too.' To this he answered 'My mammy's got a new baby.' I said that was lovely and asked the baby's name and he came off with a string of Irish boys names as long as your arm. Some followed me and helped me with my things into the taxi. One working Mum I saw said they should have this session twice a week in the summer holidays. But what about you standing there all that time with their coats waiting. 'Oh I wouldn't mind that' she said, 'Its good for them and they look forward to it each Xmas holidays.' I also thought the

Above: RTE Christmas Card 1968, watercolour on paper, 6" x 7¼", signed. RTE Dublin

schools had sent them in batches, but when I asked some of the kids were they sent by their teachers? They said, No, they read about it on the papers. No doubt James had it well publicised. When some of them asked me before I went up to start 'Are you the artist?' I said I was the binman. They said 'You're not.' 'Why not?' I asked — 'sure a binman might be an artist too. Some of their eyes popped. Then they asked me about George Campbell who had had them the day before. 'I said he was my father.' 'Crikey, he must be well over 100 years old,' they said and I replied 'Oh, yes but lots of old men and women have hearts of children,' and went on to say that I was as young as themselves in spite of my moustache and bald head. They made disbelieving eyes at this remark.

The Christmas Art Holiday which he described was an annual event for four days to enable the children to experience the artist's act of painting. As this was Gerard's first Christmas in Dublin, I, as Director of the Gallery at the time, was delighted to jump at the opportunity to get him to participate as he was a natural communicator with children. He also received an invitation in the New Year to give two weeks' tuition at the National College of Art. He thoroughly enjoyed this and the students obviously responded to his open and amusing style. He found however that the effort of preparation and then the involvement with each student left him extremely tired. At the end of the fortnight the Professor of Painting asked him if he would consider taking a part time job there. Gerard asked for time to consider but continuing health problems forced him in the end to decline.

He had recently joined the Graphic Studio with George Campbell and Arthur Armstrong and wrote with enthusiasm to his nephew, describing the technique in detail:

It's a fascinating thing altogether, roughly its this — you get a zinc or copper plate — coat it with black varnish made from beeswax and creosote — dry it and then carbon it with the flame from a candle or taper — cool it and draw on this with a sharp pointed instrument — so that that line is eaten into the plate — clear off the black wax varnish and you have an incised drawing on the plate which you can print on pre-damped paper. Clean and ink the plate so that only the incised line's depth holds the ink and put it through the press, the paper on top, and with a big wheel pull (pressure 2 tons) until the paper and plate come out the other side of the 'mangle' and the pressure pushes the paper into the inked line and, have a line drawing.

Gerard's shorthand description did not conceal the fact of the very considerable exertion involved in pulling a press two tons in pressure. In another letter he told a friend that he will 'have arm muscles on me like Tarzan.' On 19th May 1969 he wrote to his nephew:

I got a bit of a shock when I went to a heart-specialist and he said he wanted me in hospital straight away. Yet I was feeling as well as when you saw me last.

Gerard was in hospital for four weeks but made good progress and felt fit and well on his release. He had considerable success in his Dawson Gallery exhibition, selling 38 pictures and four pictures in the Belfast Arts Club group exhibition. He was able to write to his nephew on 3 July:

I'm feeling better and better and the weather is so great that I spend most of the time in the open air in the garden. The result is that I look the picture of health. Nobody would believe that I had anything wrong with me.

Poster for 'Red Roses for Me' by Sean O'Casey at the Abbey Theatre 1967/68, pen and watercolour on paper, 18" x 14"

Arthur Armstrong was a tower of strength to him during the recovery period, doing all the cooking and caring for him in every way possible and as Gerard said 'never a grumble.' No doubt his optimism was reinforced by the results of the Dawson Gallery exhibition which had sold so well and consisted of collages. This was the product of the past few years with found objects and with papers of very unusual patterns and textures which he was adapting for his own use. The mood was all the time romantic in which the sky was painted with semi-abstract shapes, sometimes suggesting the floating pierrot figures becoming clouds while the colours were pastel tones of blue, green, pink and silver as in 'Poetic Couple' (page 108) in which the background of animals, castle and vegetation suggest a stage set and the masked pierrot and seated girl are balletic in pose. In 'Shy Sweetheart' (page 94) however, the masked couple are clearly engaged in secret conversation and their attitudes suggest the overture implied in the title, whilst the background is naturalistic with a couple in a boat on the water and the strand striated with his combing technique to accentuate rhythms in contrast to the flatter quality of the collage papers used for the figures.

Apparently it was this mood of graceful figures and theatrically constructed settings which had appealed to the imagination of collectors, as well perhaps as its combination of abstraction and fantasy. For the artist himself they had opened a way for him to evoke an aspect of his beloved Western Irish landscape, now released from a direct connection with everyday feeling of the farm and fishing life of the people and the character of its inhabitants which had played so large a part in his earlier pictures, and which had been employed by many of the leading Irish painters during the past century. In this new style Gerard was inventing characters who emerged from his own imagination and desires, were influenced by his interest in ballet in his early London years, and most of all by his discovery of a way to be present as a masked pierrot in his pictures, through the works which followed the death of his brother such as 'And The Time Passes'.

Shortly afterwards he was commissioned by Dublin Regional Tourism to design a wall-hanging which he himself described as a poor man's tapestry. It is 10 by 4 feet in size and consisted of a large sheet of hessian, put together by him on the old sewing machine which Molly had got him some years earlier.

He worked twelve hours a day at it, he recorded, but would take odd days off to go over to the Graphic Studio and coming up to Christmas he made linocuts for his personal cards.

He had to walk along the quaysides to remind himself of the exact details of the Dublin skyline for the background of the wall-hanging, which represents the River Liffey with the names of the most prominent writers who were associated with it (page 108). Writing about this in the *Irish Times* on 13 March 1971 Donal Foley recorded:

> When I called on one of Ireland's leading painters recently, my first question was: Are you making your trousseau? It was reasonable enough in the context, for I had never before seen Gerard Dillon busy at a sewing-machine. Dillon's initial answer to my question is, regrettably, not publishable, but when I chased further he told me that he was working on a Wall-hanging commissioned by Dublin Regional Tourism for their head office in O'Connell Street.
>
> The result was seen last night when Rory Brugha, Alan Glynn and their colleagues gave a reception to view it. It's a very attractive synthesis of the Dublin skyline, with domes, towers, spires and trees, a suggestion of the Liffey and the names of Swift, Goldsmith, Wilde, O'Casey, W.B. Yeats, Shaw, Synge, Joyce, Beckett and Behan.
>
> 'I wanted to work Jack B. Yeats's name in since he caught so much of the essence of Dublin in a lot of his paintings but there wasn't room,' said Dillon ruefully. The artist insists on the name wall-hanging as opposed to tapestry since his technique was not the tapestry technique. The finished work is ten feet by four and Dillon used Irish rug wools, which he sewed on to a hessian base. He worked on it for eight weeks, and the main colours used are, blues, greens, yellows and purples. Gerry Dillon has played the Dublin theme before, in his poster for the Abbey production of 'Red Roses for Me' and when he collaborated with Arthur Armstrong and George Campbell in the setting for the Abbey's last production of 'Juno and The Paycock.'
>
> Though the pictorial quality of this wall-hanging is less appealing than his earlier tapestry for The Irish Tourist Board it is nevertheless a most unusual piece of decoration, taking into account that it is completely created by the use of a single treadle sewing machine and no colours or textures have been added to the natural wools.

Michael Longley, the poet who wrote 'In Memory of Gerard Dillon', and who reviewed one of his exhibitions for the *Irish Times*, has described him to me as a professional raconteur 'as well as the painter whose work has stayed with me most.' Together with Maurice Leitch, of the BBC, writer friend, he visited him during the time he was working on his wall-hanging and when the general conversation and 'crack' came round to the subject of the sewing-machine they began to invent ways whereby Gerard could use it to make a more profitable contribution to his income. All their minds were filled at this time with the proliferation of 'troubles' in the six-counties, so Gerard riposted that he would 'market loyalist knickers with the Union Jack on the behinds and up the gusset on the front he would appliqué the red hand of Ulster.'

During a visit to Belfast that Autumn, he was asked by Mr Bernard Jaffa, a dentist and collector of his works, to make a painting for the ceiling of his surgery. No doubt the general idea was to create a calm atmosphere for the patient stretched out on the operating couch below, but Mr Jaffa did not make any conditions and left it entirely to Gerard. In the event he made a large abstract which he called 'Bluescape, Greenscape' and which is 80 by 70 inches in size. This certainly is a most soothing mural and calls for no worried search from patients for themes or subjects.

The comparative calm of life in Dublin was shattered that Christmas. In the early hours of the morning Gerard was awakened by a thunderous explosion. He thought that Arthur had lifted a large chest of drawers and dropped it on the floor above him. 'I didn't know until the first news report that the O'Connell monument in the centre of Dublin had been blown up. So goodwill towards men from the UVF on Christmas night,' he wrote. Later that day he and Arthur went down to survey the damage and Gerard made a sketch of the scene. Only one winged angel was disrupted, but all the windows on the opposite side of O'Connell Street had been blown out. Because of his close involvement with Belfast, and perhaps because he was away from it, he was terribly upset by all the political commotion and disturbances to everyone's life in the North. His concentration was disrupted and he wrote to his nephew and said that he did not feel like painting but because he had a need to be creating something in colour, he was using the wool left over from the wall-hanging to make one for himself. Nevertheless he painted during the last hours of 1970 as he had always done on New Year's Eve.

In a letter to his nephew, he reported 'Arthur and I sat in and worked at art as the New Year arrived — it's an old superstition of mine that whatever I'm found doing as the New Year comes in, I'll be doing it all year.'

Illustration for 'The Vision of Mac Conglinne' by John Montague in *Ireland of the Welcomes*, vol 17 no. 1, May–June 1968. Published by the Irish Tourist Board.

12. Politics and Art

There was great feeling of buoyancy in the air for artists in the latter part of 1969. The Minister for Finance had introduced a tax amnesty for artists in every medium, living in Ireland, allowing them to be tax-free on all the profits arising from their artistic productions. It was a huge weight off the minds of artists who incurred expenses in the process of making their works. Painters and sculptors, for instance, were not likely to be good account keepers on the outlay on canvases, frames and all the various kinds of materials used and all the ancillary costs involved, which they could deduct from the sale price of works before tax was deducted. Now all these labours were eliminated and they could work without having to consider keeping accounts and knowing that the tax collector would not be asking for particulars or sending bills.

But even this good news was not enough to mollify Gerard, whose whole tenor of life had become disrupted by the continuing bad news from Belfast and the daily bulletins of strife in the North. The outbreak of religious and political bigotry in the previous year seemed to him a burden too heavy to bear and left him with a burning desire to show some support for his own kind up North. Roy Foster's *Modern Ireland* (published by Allen Lane, Penguin Press, 1988) seems to be accepted as a reasonable history. I quote from pages 587/8:

> The Northern Ireland Civil Rights Association had been founded in January 1967: by 1968 the activists among them were identifying with confrontational political tracts popular in France and America, prepared for the kind of polarization that O'Neillism tried ineffectually to defuse. Notably the radical People's Democracy movement, born in the crucible of student revolt, adopted the tactics of civil disobedience: media attention would assure leaders like Bernadette Devlin worldwide prominence. The analogies with student movements elsewhere are easy to make. But sociologists invariably observe the absence of a distinct 'youth culture' in Ulster society: young people there are more likely to identify with traditionalist, adult-dominated activities within their own communities. Given the presence of new look socialist republicans among the civil rights activists, and the origin of

> several of their tactics in discussions of the Wolfe Tone society, the results were predictable. When elements among the People's Democracy flew the republican tricolour, they claimed it symbolised Orange and Green united within Ulster. To Protestant observers, already insecure, it represented a less arcane identification. To them, civil rights demonstrations meant that the republican fifth column was on the march again.

> The allocation of housing became the flashpoint — though, ironically, levels of inequity were no longer as spectacular as claimed. In 1968, occupations, squattings, marches, might appear the simple mechanics of the international student protest; but within Ulster they represented symbolic invasion of ancient territory, and the assertion of an illegitimate right to 'walk'. And the forces of the Protestant state reacted accordingly. Violence began at a Derry march in October 1968, notably on the part of the police — Royal Ulster Constabulary as well as B-specials. A percussion of violence was set off by the ambush of marchers by Paisleyites at Burntollet Bridge in January 1969, culminating in the terrible 'Battle of the Bogside' in August, and the subsequent onslaught by Protestant mobs and the B-specials on Catholic areas of Belfast. Troops were already being used in aid of the civil power — but reluctantly. They were now fully committed. The Belfast violence left ten dead, 1,600 injured and property damage of £8,000,000.

Having grown up in an atmosphere where Catholic, nationalist views were regarded as inviolable, Gerard was already able to see only one side of the picture. However, having come to live in Dublin, he was now getting the news through a Southern Irish newspaper and TV point of view and it was even more clear now in his eyes that the happenings in the North were outrageous. He wrote to his nephew:

> God, my blood boiled as I watched the suffering of people in the Bogside (Now an honourable name to be remembered). I felt worse when I saw how the B-specials devastated the streets around the back of Clonard Street. I felt it so much that I sat down and wrote the following to the *Irish Times*.

On 20 August 1969 his letter was published:

> Sir, As a personal gesture and as an individual artist I am withdrawing my work from The Irish Exhibition of Living Art after it is shown in Cork city. The exhibition which opens in Cork on Wednesday is scheduled for a month's showing in Belfast. I feel too that every artist worthy of the name should make his public protest against the persecution of the Irish people by a planter Government in the Six Counties of Ulster. I would also suggest that the entire exhibition should not go to the North, and that a protest note should be sent to the Arts Council of Northern Ireland,

who are to house this exhibition in October. It is sad to think that the capital city has not been able to provide a gallery to show this work.

Being an Irishman and an Ulsterman, I know only too well the arrogance of that Unionist mob who think it is their right to rule the Irish people with the jackboot. They have such brass that they honestly think that the Irish should leave their homeland to them. It would never occur to them that it would be the decent thing, and an easy thing, to arrange with that racial specialist in their own party, Enoch Powell, who would welcome them home or could arrange their fares to join their other kith and kin in Rhodesia. They'd be past masters helping Ian Smith and his like mob of power-crazy gangsters in stamping the black people of that unhappy country into the dust.

Recently the Arts Council of Northern Ireland invited me to join two other Irish artists, one living in the North and the other here in Dublin, in a three-man touring exhibition of the North. To this invitation, I've answered that I could not allow my work to go up there while the Rev. Ian Paisley remains Prime Minister and encourages his Government to persecute my fellow-Irishmen.

I hope my fellow artists protest in some way. Yours etc., Gerard Dillon. Ranelagh, Dublin 6.

In his letter to his nephew, Gerard also stated that for the first time he could say he was glad that his brother Joe was dead and not living alone with his little dog in the old family home. But other relatives and friends still lived in this area and Gerard saw it all as part of his past, particularly associated with the unbelievably bitter religious and political discrimination under which he grew up. It is true that he and other members of his family ran away out of this atmosphere of bitterness. But for an artist of extreme sensitivity who was not only unable to tolerate violence of any kind but could not bear to think of the Crucifixion of Christ, which was so cardinal a part of his family's religious ceremonies, the effect of the present happenings were concentrated and cumulative. His letter to the *Irish Times* was an opening for him to take part in some way in what he felt was the sacrifice of his own people. As the emotional type he was, he was not satisfied to make his protest but must also use the occasion to vent himself of bitter feelings. On 20 August, the IELA opened in Cork and the committee chartered a train to take exhibitors and others interested to the opening. There were some 130 persons on the train including 30 exhibitors. Having prepared a hard-covered notebook with the following preliminary statement, Gerard presented it to each passenger.

Proposal for a Public Protest in the Press.

We the undersigned propose that the Irish Exhibition of Living Art should make a public protest against the persecution of Irish People by the present Stormont Government, by withholding this year's exhibition from the Arts Council of Northern Ireland which had planned to show it in Belfast after it leaves Cork. And that the Living Art should give a lead in this and encourage all cultural bodies in Ireland to protest in every way and any form against the horror that the Stormont Government has inflicted on the Irish People. Anything that will make the Stormont Government appear respectable should be denied them.

108 of those on the train signed the statement though subsequently three of them withdrew their names. Amongst the signatories were 25 exhibitors. Naturally Gerard's proposal was a difficult one, since it meant that artists, by refusing to allow their work to be exhibited, were taking the risk that they might be losing sales, and such exhibitions were the principal means of providing them with a living.

At the public opening in Cork on Thursday 21 August, Michael Farrell, one of the most distinguished of the Irish painters made a strong statement aligning himself with Dillon's protest and stating that he would not let his work go to be shown in a gallery supported by that regime. He had won an award of £300 at that year's exhibition and he was going to give part of the money to an artist's fund.

Following the Dillon letter, a long correspondence developed in the letters pages of the main Irish newspapers and leading articles were devoted to the subject. The general consensus seemed to be summed up in an *Irish Times* leader which said:

Art transcends the passions of humanity and knows no frontiers. It is, at its best, a form of evangelism, a truth that helps to make men free, and Belfast and the North need truth and freedom in all walks of its life. The art life of Dublin has been enriched by painters from Ulster; some of them work down here; most of them show their work down here. Without them we would be the poorer. Whatever divides us politically or religiously, art should be one of the healers. It should be above the battle.

On Monday 25 August, a committee meeting of IELA was held and Gerard appended the following note in the book of signatures collected on the train:

This meeting was amiable enough and we talked a lot. It ended up by the majority voting that the Living Art were in complete sympathy with the exhibitors who protested and the ones who wished to withdraw their work from the show at the end of the exhibition in Cork. That they abhorred the Unionist Party's actions in recent times but thought that they should keep their promise and send the exhibition to Belfast. (The names of those present were then entered and the fact that they voted). But the fact that they were making this public statement about the Stormont Government's treatment of people in the North has achieved something. They would never have done this had I not created the situation which forced this out of them.

The statement which appeared in the press had been modified after the meeting according to Gerard's record. The committee had agreed, he understood, to express sympathy with those who had suffered. Otherwise it was in accordance with what had been agreed. It read:

> The committee of the Irish Exhibition of Living Art has considered a request from some artists and their friends that the exhibition should not be shown in Belfast after its current showing in Cork, as a protest against recent actions of the Unionist Government of Northern Ireland. Some artists have also indicated their intentions of withdrawing their works from the exhibition if it goes to Belfast.

> The committee has the fullest sympathy with the genuine feeling that has prompted the action of these artists. Nevertheless the committee believes that it should keep its agreement with the North of Ireland's Arts Council for the exhibition to be shown in Belfast. The committee has always enjoyed the support of artists from all parts of Ireland, and believes that maintaining such links is especially important at this tragic time.

Gerard continued to make notes in this book which he carefully preserved, presumably as a record of the failure of his artist friends to stand together to make the strong protest he hoped for. Personally he felt a strong sense of satisfaction in the fact that he had taken an active part on behalf of Northern nationalists through the only way of life that seemed relevant and important to him. For some considerable time afterwards, he felt that many of his colleagues in IELA 'cold shouldered' him. Much of this feeling was imagined for he knew he had disturbed many of his close friends who in no way shared his background and beliefs. In time he came round to the importance of IELA for him — with all its associations, and he kept his place on the committee. He showed two of his new paintings at the 1970 IELA which that year was held in the National Gallery of Ireland. These were 'Red Nude with Loving Pierrot' and 'Grey Nude with Loving Pierrot'. In a letter to his nephew in April 1970, he reported:

I've worked hard and painted every day. The new paintings are oils using the nude drawings I did in London, trying to make interesting pictures; combing the nudes. They are lovely colours and Smith liked them tho' said they wouldn't sell. That means my next show might be a flop. But that's how it goes. But its a long way off and maybe by that time I may have developed further — who knows?

In fact he had been using the nudes made at the Sarah Siddons school before he left London and one suspects that his regular attendances at the Graphic Studios removed the urge he normally experienced to find new subjects in nature. In paintings like 'Once Upon a Wavelength' (page 107) he had combined the seated nude figure with the forms in the sky which twist and swirl in the red clouds. Beneath these and just above the head of the clown in the boat, a separate nude figure floats as if released from the earth below. During 1970 he was deeply involved with mastering the various graphic techniques and by contrast on his days off from printing he painted very freely with bright colours and seemed to enter a dream world of escape from the present.

Such works as 'Red Nude with Loving Pierrot' (page 107) or 'Clown Painting Nude' probably represent his most lyrical phase of painting and one in which he came nearest to a truly poetic expression of his desires for pictures far removed from the realities and pains of daily life, and indeed in no way reminiscent of the Northern conflict which was never far from his mind. He also exhibited, in that year's RHA exhibition, four variations of these nude studies which continued to reflect this mood and in strong contrast to the products of previous years when he was always fired by the excitement of conquering new methods and mediums not formerly part of his artistic experience. One of his last pictures, 'The Painters Dilemma' (cover, and page 110) captured what was probably his sense of uncertainty about life after death. The artist is seated in a large space and in the depths behind are placed symbols of life's alternatives — the Crucifixion group beneath the menacing bird-angel. On the opposite side a sex symbol and in between the picture awaiting completion if he only had the answer.

He was asked by Leo Smith of the Dawson Gallery to prepare an exhibition of his early works of the West of Ireland for the following March 1971. This was followed in April 1971 by an exhibition of a more widespread collection of his works of all periods, in the Tom Caldwell

Gallery in Belfast, and also included were three of the etchings recently produced.

In the process of arranging his Belfast exhibition Gerard decided to go up to stay with his old friend Tom Davidson. Tom was conscious that Gerard looked poorly but nevertheless could not persuade him to go to bed and he insisted on talking on into the early hours. Next morning Tom discovered that Gerard had had a stroke and his mouth was clenched so that he could hardly talk. They had him removed to hospital and after a couple of weeks he was taken by ambulance to Dublin. Although handicapped in his speech his ability to express himself was in no way impaired and he wrote to his nephew:

> The journey by ambulance was very good, they put hot water bottles around me in the stretcher. Although it was a beautiful sunny morning it was cold. And I was right about the glass (window) — tho' it looks blank from outside, you can see out clearly. We were not stopped at either border post. We didn't stop for a meal as the hospital had made it up for me, and I showed the nurses how to use the tube feeder.

Madge Connolly, his old friend and confidante, had come over from London and was at the Adelaide Hospital waiting to greet him on arrival in Dublin. He settled into the new routine and was visited by numbers of his friends. He himself wrote that because of his vanity he dreaded the concern they showed in their faces for the clenched condition of his jaw. There was much to please him, however. He sold all 29 pictures in the Dawson Gallery exhibition and several others from stock and later Tom Caldwell announced that he had already sold 20 works in Belfast. He showed some improvement so Madge and Dr Maura McQuaid made arrangements to take him over to London in order that he could have rehabilitation treatment in Camden Town. His nephew Gerard planned to come down to Dublin and to accompany him on the journey to London. This sudden new turn of events absolutely thrilled him after some three months in hospital and he was excited by the prospect of meeting once again all his old London friends. However, before the plan could be put into operation he had another stroke and he died on 14th June 1971. And his last wishes were carried out. He was buried 'in a real, old, untidy, Belfast graveyard. I have no wish to be buried in a little, prissy, English graveyard with everything in neat little headstones.'

On 21 July, some five weeks later, the IELA opened in the National Gallery of Ireland and subsequently in the Arts Council Gallery in Belfast. A group of his paintings was given a place of honour as memorial to him. In the catalogue, I wrote this tribute:

> He was the clown in his own pictures always fully involved in the business of living. Optimistic and lyrical, he found his subjects in people's courage and resilience. In spite of poverty in his Belfast youth, and privation in his days of house painting and janitoring in London, he was never daunted and knew exactly where he was going. He was going to be a painter. 'If people don't buy my pictures, more fool they,' one can still hear his challenging Northern voice.
>
> Gerard Dillon knew that the way to make a work of art was to pluck the image hot out of experience and to set it down in whatever colour, shape or form he found responsive to the available materials. Again and again I found him at work with all sorts of unexpected things. At one time he mixed sand with his paint and baked the whole picture for hours in his gas oven. At another he adapted a sewing machine for making stitch patterning over appliqued cloth and this led to the 'poor man's' tapestries which he made with coloured wools darned into hessian.
>
> The lack of money was never an obstacle to him, rather the reverse. He was surrounded by rejected objects like old leather handbags or gloves which he washed and cut up and turned into splendid birds flying across his landscapes or witches' brooms with which he would beat back the forces of reaction in life — the only hate he permitted himself. Which thought recalls the brave way he went around London collecting money for the committee which led to the far reaching changes after the Wolfenden report. He was both a complete artist and a wonderfully humane man who never grew old. Everyone in the world of art, especially living art, loved him dearly and will mourn him always.

Shortly after he died, Arthur Armstrong asked John Kelly, the Director of the Graphic Studio, what he should do about the more than 50 plates which Gerard had etched. John explained that these should be cancelled by scratching an X across each plate so that if anyone tried to print it this mark would show.

John Kelly had been immensely impressed by Gerard's application and industry when he came with Arthur and George Campbell to commence work in the Graphic Studio more than a year previous to his last illness.

> He has made 'some four dozen copper plates for etching' [John told me], 'I was proofing the last one when I heard that he had had a stroke. Gerard never made a drawing for his plate. He would wax it — smoke it black, take up a needle and literally sit down and start drawing. The reason why etching appealed

Magic in the Sky, oil on canvas, 30"x34", signed. Exhibited IELA 1968. PC

Above: *Cut out, Drop out*, oil on canvas, 36"x47". Exhibited IELA 1968. AIB Art Collection
Facing page top: *Once upon a Wavelength*, oil on canvas, 40"x60", signed.
Exhibited 'Ulster Painting' 1968 Arts Council of Northern Ireland. Taylor Galleries Dublin
Facing page bottom: *Red Nude with Loving Pierrot*, oil on canvas 36"x48". Exhibited IELA 1970. Taylor Galleries Dublin

Above: *Poetic Couple*, oil and collage on panel, 22"x31". Exhibited Dawson Gallery 1969. PC
Below: Dublin Wall Hanging, stitched, appliqued and machine and hand woven on Hessian,
48"x120", 1971. Dublin Regional Tourist Board, Irish Tourist Board
Facing page: *Boy and Small Fields*, etching on paper, artist's proof, 13½" x 9½". 1970

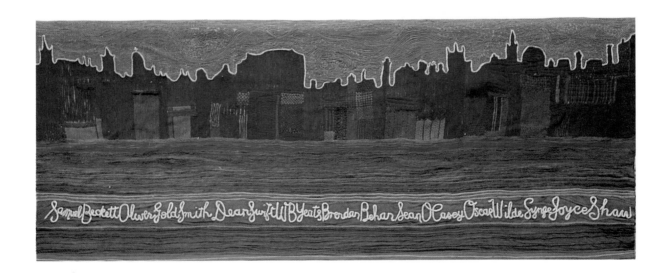

to him — he carried the image in his mind and he would draw it directly unlike all other artists who worked from drawings. Once he discovered etching, it became clear that it was exactly what he had been looking for. When he put the image on the plate, he would take the proof and he would colour it in and develop it to a certain stage; then he would redraw on top of the plate again. He always had the basic image in his mind — he would add in another figure, then change it, then put an arm in or change the tree; because the image was in his mind of what he wanted to produce. It was a great shame he did not have access to a studio before — he was of all the artists I have taught the most natural. He turned out works by the dozen in a short space of time. Gerry was very deceptive, a very funny man. On the surface appeared a very casual approach to what he was doing but he was deadly serious. He had a very light touch in his treatment of his work and I believed that if he had discovered etching earlier he would have developed a great command and been quite extraordinary. He crammed into a year a phenomenal output.

Once Gerard discovered that he could shade a figure or make it disappear, he wanted to go on all day changing. He had the natural approach — curiosity. He would have been a super film maker. Sequential images came naturally to him. He never made any preparations. He simply sat down, started to draw and one thing suggested another. He wanted to alter each image and make 20 different pictures from one.

John Kelly summed him up as 'innocent — such incredible knowledge — most sophisticated — underneath, always funny, always childlike.' He also told John Kelly that he would put his pictures at the foot of his bed so that when he woke up in the morning, in the cold light of day, he could decided whether or not they were any good. Either he would say 'My God, Dillon, you're a good painter' or he would destroy them.

If, as is probable, the strenuous work of the Graphic Studio hastened his end, he would have had no regrets. He lived his life in pursuit of his art and let nothing stand in its way. As he grew older, this became more apparent. During those last few years in Dublin, his appetite for social activities and being the organiser of the songs and recitations at the parties began to diminish because he was saving his energies for print-making and painting. He had forecast that he would not live more than 55 years. Nor did he. But up to his last day, he wrote letters to his friends and illustrated them with drawings of himself in the bed or trying to cope with learning to walk and get around. It is hard to imagine that any other artist ever got more out of his art than Gerard did. Through it he discovered the full joy of creativity.

The Painter's Dilemma, oil on canvas, 48"x48", signed. PC

Appendix One

Group Exhibitions

1 Gaelic League Golden Jubilee Exhibition, 1943. 7 Pictures, 1 Sculpture. St Mary's Minor Hall, Bank St., Belfast. 19th to 29th May.

2 Contemporary Pictures Gallery, 133 Lr. Baggot St., Dublin. 18 Oils, 19 W.C.s. Exhibition by Gerard Dillon and Daniel O'Neill. December 1943.

3 John Lamb Gallery, 25 Bridge St., Portadown. 30 Pictures. Exhibition by Gerard Dillon and George F. Campbell. June-July 1944.

4 William Moll Gallery, Queen St. Belfast. No Catalogue. 1944. Progressive Group (Dan O'Neill, George Campbell, John Turner, Gerard Dillon.)

5 CEMA Northern Ireland. Ormeau Ave., Belfast. 2 Pictures. Works by Some Ulster Artists. 1944-45.

6 The Leicester Galleries, Leicester Sq., London. 4 Pictures. Living Irish Art and New Sculptures and drawings by Henry Moore. October 1946.

7 Associated American Artists Galleries, 5th Ave., New York. Also Chicago. March 1947. (Catalogue not traced.)

8 Victor Waddington Galleries, 8 Sth Anne St., Dublin. 7 Pictures. Recent Paintings by Campbell, Dillon, Johnston and O'Neill. September 1947.

9 Heals, Mansard Gallery, 1959 Tottenham Court Rd., London. 8 Pictures. Four Ulster Painters. May-June 1948.

10 Irish Painters in Holland. 2 Pictures. Instituut Nederland — Ierland. Amsterdam, Rotterdam 1949.

11 CEMA Northern Ireland, Belfast. 16 Pictures. Paintings by Allen Adams and Gerard Dillon. December 1949.

12 Gimpel Fils, 84 Duke St., London W1. 1 Oil. De Lumine et Colore. Summer Exhibition 1949.

13 New Irish Painters, Institute of Contemporary Arts, Boston. 1950.

14 Scottish Arts Council, Edinburgh, Aberdeen, Dundee, Ayr, Arbroath. 3 Oils. Contemporary Ulster Paintings. January 1951.

15 Arthur Tooth and Sons Ltd., 31 Bruton St., London W1. 6 Oils. Five Irish Painters. May-June 1951.

16 Childs Gallery, 169 Newberry St.. Boston. 6 Oils. Three Irish Painters. January-February 1952.

17 Cultural Relations Committee Exhibition of Irish Artists in Gothenberg and Stockholm 1952. 4 Oils.

18 CEMA Northern Ireland, Belfast. 'The Fish Eaters.' C.E.M.A. Collection of Ulster Artists. September 1952.

19 Victor Waddington Galleries, Dublin. 2 Oils. Summer Exhibition. July-August 1953.

20 Municipal Gallery of Modern Art, Dublin. 2 Oils. An Tostal, Irish Paintings from Private Collection. 1953.

21 Goodwin Gallery, Limerick. No catalogue available. Six Irish Painters. 1953.

22 An Tostal, Bray, Co Wicklow. 3 Oils. International Hotel, Bray. April-May 1954.

23 Cultural Relations Committee Exhibition of Irish Artists in Germany 5 oils. 1955.

24 Royal Institute London. Group Exhibition. No catalogue available. 1955.

25 Piccadilly Gallery, London. Works by George Campbell and Gerard Dillon. No catalogue available. June 1955.

26 Irish Club, Eaton Square, London. Works by George Campbell and Gerard Dillon. No catalogue available. July-August 1955.

27 Victor Waddington Galleries, Dublin. 30 Years. Group Exhibition. 2 Oils. February 1956.

28 Graves Gallery, Sheffield. Contemporary Art in Ulster. 5 Oils. 1957.

29 Guggenheim International Exhibition, New York. 'Seabeast Basking' chosen. 1958.

30 Belfast Museum and Art Gallery. Lewinter Frankl collection. 2 Oils. March-April 1958.

31 Carnegie Prize Exhibition. Carnegie Institute, Pittsburgh. 35 British Artists. 'Ascelt Group' by Gerard Dillon chosen. Dec. 1958-Feb. 1959.

32 Guggenheim International Exhibition. New York. 'Masquerade' chosen. 1960.

33 CEMA New Gallery Belfast, Opened 25th June 1960. 3 Oils. 1960.

34 Marzotto International, Rome. 'The Side of A Hill' chosen. 1961.

35 Raymond Duncan Gallery, Paris. No Catalogue available. 1961.

36 The First Group. South London Art Gallery, Henry Anderson, Gerard Dillon. Stanley Pinker, Ken Turner, Sally Anderson. May 1961.

37 Gallery 25, Brunswick Street, London. Gerard Dillon and George Campbell. 18 Pictures. 1962.

38 Savage Gallery, London. Eight Irish Artists. Catalogue Not Available. 1962.

39 Festival of Modern International Art Boston. Catalogue not Available. 1962. Also at Obelisk Gallery, Washington.

40 Marzotto International, Rome. 'In The Swirl of The Blue Wind' chosen. 1963. (Also at Whitechapel Gallery, London.)

41 New School for Social Research, Wollman Hall, New York. 12 Irish Artists. In conjunction with Lord and Taylors Promotion. 6 Oils. 1963.

42 Municipal Gallery of Modern Art, Dublin. Paintings from Private Collections. 3 Oils. 1965.

43 Eight Northern Painters, New Charing Cross Gallery, Glasgow. 1966.

44 Ulster Painting '68. Arts Council Gallery, Belfast. 2 Pictures. 1968.

45 Ulster Arts Club, Belfast. Paintings by Gerard Dillon and Arthur Armstrong. 1969.

46 Independent Artists, Municipal Gallery of Modern Art, Dublin. 1969.

47 The Irish Imagination 1959-1971. Municipal Gallery of Modern Art, Dublin, 1971. 1 Oil. Oct-Dec 1971.

48 Belfast Schools Art Collection. Arts Council of Northern Ireland, Gallery. 1973.

49 Limerick City Library Gallery. Paintings from The Collection of An Comhairle Ealaoin. 1973.
50 Rosc, Irish Art 1900-1950. 1 Oil. Cork 1975/76.
51 Rosc, Irish Art 1943-1973. Cork and Belfast. 1980/81.
52 Belltable Arts Centre Limerick. A Personal Choice, 1981. 1 Painting.
53 A Century of Connemara. Galway Arts Festival, 1984. 3 Oils.

Royal Hibernian Academy

(Year and Title of picture exhibited)
1943. 'Disused Brickfields.'
1952. 'Connemara Child.'
1958. 'Rocky Island Shore.'
       'Interior with Figures.'
1959. 'A Net of Fields.'
       'Turning The Earth.'
1965. 'Clown with Birds.'
       'Model and Canvas.'
1966. 'Clown with Red Lady.'
       'Irish Forms.'
       'Sea Drift.'
1968. 'Artist's Dilemma.'
       'Couple on The Rocks.'
       'Dreaming.'
       'His Two Selves.'
1969. 'Wren Boys.'
       'Artists Light.'
1970. 'Pink Nude.'
       'Green Nude.'
1971. 'People in Their World.'
       'Waiting and Watching.'

Irish Exhibition of Living Art

1943. 'Black Eyes.'
       'Crucified City.'
1944. 'Cemetery Sunday.'
       'Blast.'
       'The Blue Pool.'
       'Potato Pickers.'
1946   (At the Leicester Gallery London in 1946.)

'Couple from Inishmaan.'
'The Well.'
'Dust to Dust.'
'Aran Funeral.'
1947. 'Cursing Tinkers.'
       'Picnic.'
       'A Sea of Bracken.'
1948. 'Gossiping Boys.'
1949. 'Procession in Tuscany.'
       'Memory Pool.'
       'Italian with Fowl.'
1950. 'Goat Herd.'
       'Fast Day.'
       'St Francis.'
1951. 'Cattle and Crows.'
       'The Scholars.'
       'Corpus Christi, Roundstone.'
       'Lobster Pots.'
1952. 'Spanish Village Fair.'
       'Bull Fight.'
       'Caves outside Granada.'
1953. 'Island Tapestry.'
       'Red Attic.'
       'Gentle Breeze.' (tapestry)
       'The Dung Hill.'
1955. 'Self Contained Flat.'
       'Inishlackan Couple.'
       'Tea Party.'
       'Little Girl's Wonder.'
1956. 'The Old Woman.'
       'Shipping The Cattle.'
       'Three Men in A Bog.'
       'The White Rocks.'
1957. 'Children and Chalk.'
       'The Dreamer.'
       'The End.'
       'The Tinker Family.'
1958. 'Any Old Irish Town.'
       'Goodbye Old Paint.'
       'Not Fish nor Fowl.'
1959. 'Abstract Composition.'
       'Birds Watching.'
       'Black Art.'
       'Composition White Hen.'
1960. 'Moon Flower.'
       'The Honoured Cord.'
       'Look at Me.'
       'One and One is One.'
1961. 'Beast Bird.'
       'The Soul of A Slipper Beatle.'
       'Shore Bird.'
       'Sack, Sealing Wax and String.'
1962. 'A Bird's World.'
       'Harvest Image.'

Appendix Two

'Spider's Heaven.'
'Space Circus.'
1963 'Sea Beast Basking.'
'Expanding Form.'
'Bagdad.'
'Ascelt Form.'
1964. 'An Awesome Place.'
'Cool Water.'
'A Green Place.'
'Totem and Waste Land.'
1965. 'Masked Figure and Nude.'
'Pierrot and Picture.'
'Hypnotic Mask.'
'Mask and Canvas.'
1966. 'Red Profile and Canvas.'
'Wandering through Life.'
'Head, Canvas and Still Life.'
1967. 'Looking Back.'
'The Brothers.'
'Resting Place.'
1968. 'Cut Out, Drop Out.'
'Magic in The Sky.'
'Red Sky Wonder.'
1969. 'Green Space.'
'Red and Silver Planes.'
1970. 'Red Nude with Loving Pierrot.'
'Grey Nude with Loving Pierrot.'
1971. Memorial Exhibition of 11
paintings included.

One-Man Exhibitions

1942. The Country Shop, St Stephens Green, Dublin.
1946. The Arts Council of Northern Ireland, Belfast.
1950. The Victor Waddington Galleries, Dublin.
1950. The Arts Council of Northern Ireland, Belfast.
1953. The Victor Waddington Galleries, Dublin.
1954. The Maxwell Galleries, 372 Suter St., San Francisco, 8.
1954. Drogheda Art Gallery. Exhibition of Watercolours.
1956. CEMA Gallery, 55A, Donegal Place, Belfast.
1957. The Dawson Gallery, Dublin.
1958. The Queen's University Gallery, Belfast.
1959. The Dawson Gallery, Dublin.
1960. The Dawson Gallery, Dublin.
1962. The Dawson Gallery, Dublin.
1963. The Dawson Gallery, Dublin.
1965. The Dawson Gallery, Dublin.
1966. The Arts Council of Northern Ireland Gallery, Belfast.
1966. The Dawson Gallery, Dublin.
1967. The Mercury Gallery, London.
1968. The Dawson Gallery, Dublin.
1969. The Dawson Gallery, Dublin.
1971. The Dawson Gallery, Dublin.
1971. The Tom Caldwell Gallery, 56 Bradbury Place, Belfast, 7

Appendix Three

Published Writings

Envoy. A monthly magazine published by The Envoy Publishing Co. Ltd., 39 Grafton St., Dublin. Vol. 4., No 15., February 1955. Pages 39/40. Gerard Dillon contributes to a Symposium 'The Artist Speaks.'

Ireland of The Welcomes. A monthly magazine published by Bord Failte Eireann, Baggot Street Bridge, Dublin 2. Vol 4. May/June 1955. Pages 30 to 33. Gerard Dillon writes and illustrates 'Dear Tourist' a letter from a painter.

The Artist a quarterly magazine published by the Artist Publishing Co., 51 Piccadilly, London W1 vol 53, No 1. March 1957 pages 16/18. Gerard writes and illustrates 'Unusual Media' 1. The Importance of Drawing.

The Artist. Vol 53., No 2. April 1957 Pages 41/3. Gerard Dillon writes and illustrates 'Unusual Media' 11. Collages.

The Artist. Vol 53., No 3, May 1957 Pages 68/70. Gerard Dillon writes and illustrates 'Unusual Media' 111. Monotype.

Ireland of The Welcomes. Vol 13. No 2. July/Aug 1964. Pages 8/11. Gerard Dillon writes and illustrates 'Connemara is Ireland to Me.'

Gramophone Recording

Pye Group Record N.P.L. 18028. 'Ottiline's Irish Night.' Includes songs sung by Gerard Dillon, 'I know My Love' and 'Cailin Deas.'

Publications with Illustrations Only

An Tostal, Official Souvenir Handbook. Published Fogra Failte, Dublin, 1953. Full page illustration 'The Irish at Play' and 2 thumbnail sketches.

The Radio Times, London, Dec. 1955. 'The Return Room', (a Backwindow on Belfast opened after forty years) by W.R. Rodgers. b/w drawing.

One Small Boy, by Bill Naughton, MacGibbon and Kee, London. Jacket Design by Gerard Dillon.

Ireland of the Welcomes. Vol. 5 No. 4, Nov-Dec 1956. 'Connemara comehither' by Thomas Kelly, three b/w illustrations.

Ireland of the Welcomes. Vol. 6 No. 1. May-June 1957. 'Horse Racing on The Strand' by Lally Bourke. Six b/w illustrations.

Ireland of the Welcomes. Vol. 6 No. 2. July-August 1957. 'Walking The Farm' by Stephen Rynne. Six b/w illustrations.

Ireland of the Welcomes. Vol. 7 No. 3. Sept-Oct. 1958. 'The Dingle Peninsula' by Brian Fitzgerald. Three b/w illustrations.

Bord Failte Christmas Card for 1964.

Ireland of the Welcomes. Vol. 13. No. 4. Nov-Dec 1964. Christmas Card for Failte reproduced in colour on cover.

UNICEF Christmas Card for 1966.

Ireland of the Welcomes. Vol. 17 No. 1 May-June 1968. 'The Vision of MacConglinne' by John Montague. Three b/w illustrations.

Ireland of the Welcomes. Vol. 17 No. 4. Nov-Dec 1968. 'Irish Blessings' by John B. Keane. Five b/w illustrations.

Telefis Eireann Christmas Card for 1968.

Ireland of the Welcomes. Vol. 19 No. 3. Sept-Oct 1970. 'Irish Curses' by John B. Keane. Six b/w illustrations.

Bibliography

1943. *Irish Art Handbook*. Cahill & Co., Dublin 1943. Independent Painters by James White.

1943. *Ulster in Black and White*. 16 Pages of Drawings by George Campbell, Arthur Campbell, Patricia Webb and Maurice Wilks. 8 Royal Terrace, Lisburn Rd., Belfast.

1944. *Irish Art*. The Parkside Press, Cahill & Co., Dublin, 1944. Pictures for The Home by James White.

1944. *Now in Ulster*. Compiled by George Campbell and Arthur Campbell. 3/6. Printed by W. & G. Baird, Ltd., Belfast. Some Ulster Artists by John Hewitt. 1 Painting and 4 Thumbnail sketches by Dillon reproduced.

1949. *Art News and Review*, London, March 1949. Letter from Dublin by James White.

1951. *Envoy*, Dublin, Feb. 1951. See published writings, Appendix 1.

1951. *The Arts in Ulster*. A Symposium by Sam Hanna Bell, Nesca A. Robb, John Hewitt. Geo G. Harrap and Co. Ltd, London. 1951. Pages 91/2.

1952. *The Tablet*, London. March 29th 1952. The Dublin Scene by Derek Patmore.

1953. *An Tostal*. Official Souvenir Handbook, 5th to 26th April 1953. The Visual Arts in Ireland by James White. 'Omey Island Strand' by Gerard Dillon reproduced.

1955. *Studies*, Dublin. Spring 1955. The Visual Arts in Ireland by James White.

1955. *Irische Kunst der Gegenwart*. Iserlohn, Holland. 1955. Introduction by James White.

1955. *Ireland of The Welcomes*. May, June 1955. Painting and Sculpture by Arland Ussher.

1955,6. *The Artist*. See published writings, Appendix 1.

1958. Mainie Jellett, *The Artist's Vision*. The Dundalgan Press, Ltd., W Tempest, Dundalk. Edited Eileen McCarvill. Introduction by Albert Gleizes. 1958.

1959. *Merian (Irland)*. Hoffman und Kampe Verlag, Hamburg 1959. Kontakt mit um Kontinent by James White.

1962. *Doctrine and Life*. October 1962. Vol 12. No 10. Dominican Publications, Dublin 1. Comment on 'The Crowning with Thorns' and reproduction of painting by James White.

1963. *Ireland by the Irish*. Galley Press, Ltd., London, 1963 edited by Michael Gorman. The Irishman Sees by James White.

1966. Arts Council of Northern Ireland, Belfast. *Gerard Dillon Exhibition Catalogue*. Introduction by James White.

1967. The Mercury Gallery London. *Gerard Dillon Exhibition Catalogue*. Introduction by James White.

1968. *Encyclopedia of Ireland*, Allen Figgis, Dublin 1968. 'Paintings' by James White. Page 337.

1968. *Concise History of Irish Art*, Bruce Arnold. Praeger, New York 1968, Thames and Hudson, London 1969.

1969. *Eire-Ireland*, Dublin. Modern Art in Ireland by Hilary Pyle.

1971. The Dawson Gallery, Dublin. *Gerard Dillon Exhibition of Early Paintings of The West*. Introduction by James White.

1971. *Causeway*, The Arts in Ulster. Edited Michael Longley. Gill and Macmillan and The Arts Council of Northern Ireland, 1971. Painting and Sculpture by Kenneth Jamison, Pages 45/6 and repro.

1971. *The Irish Imagination 1959-1971*. Catalogue of the Exhibition in Municipal Gallery of Modern Art, Dublin in Oct. 1971. Introduction by Brian O'Doherty, Biography by Christopher Fitzsimon.

1972. *Gerard Dillon, A Retrospective Exhibition 1916-1971*. Ulster Museum, Belfast, Nov-Dec 1972, Municipal Gallery of Modern Art, Dublin, Dublin, Jan-Feb 1973. Introduction by James White, Biography by Noreen Rice.

1972. *Balcony of Europe*, Aidan Higgins. Calder & Boyars, London, 1972.

1974. *Apollo*, London, May 1974, Aspects of Irish Art by Brian Fallon.

1976. *Irish Art 1900-1950*. Catalogue of the Exhibition at The Crawford Municipal Art Gallery, Cork by Hilary Pyle, Dec 1975–Jan 1976.

1976. *Art History and Appreciation*, James Burns, School and College Services, Dublin 4, 1976. Page 49 and repro.

1977. *Art in Ulster 1*, John Hewitt. Blackstaff Press, Ltd, Upper Newtownards Road, Belfast, BT4 3JF. 1977 with biography by Theo Snoddy and repro.

1977 *Art in Ulster 2*, Mike Catto. Blackstaff Press Ltd., Belfast. 1977 with biography by Theo Snoddy and repro.

1978. *The Honest Ulsterman*. See published writings.

1980. *Irish Art 1943-1973*. Catalogue of the Exhibition in The Crawford Municipal Art Gallery, Cork, Aug-Nov 1980, Ulster Museum, Belfast, Jan-Feb 1981, by Cyril Barrett, S.J.

1982. *The Arts in Ireland, A Chronology*, Christopher Fitzsimon. Gill and Macmillan, Dublin 8, 1982. Pages 188, 210, 224, 234, 240.

1983. *Ireland, A Cultural Encyclopedia*. Edited Brian de Breffny, Thames and Hudson, London. 1983. Biography by Ciaran McGonigal and repro.

1984. *Ireland and The Arts*. Edited Tim Pat Coogan. Namara Press, London 1984. Page 200.

1984. *Concise Catalogue of The Drawings and Paintings in The Ulster Museum 1984*. Page 31.

1984. *Modern Irish Landscape Painting*, Frances Ruane. The Arts Councils in Ireland, Dublin and Belfast. 1984. Biography and Transparency.

1986. *Allied Irish Banks Collection*, Douglas Hyde Gallery and Allied Irish Banks 1986. by Frances Ruane, Biography and 2 repros.

1986. *The Sketchbooks of Picasso*. Thames and Hudson, London 1986. Picasso at The Crossroads by Theodore Reff.

1987. *The Irish Messenger*. 37 Lr. Leeson Street, Dublin, 2. 'Figures in Connemara landscape' (Gerard Dillon) by Marie Bourke.

1988. *National Gallery of Ireland, Acquisitions 1986-1988*. Introduction by Adrian le Harivel, and repro.

1988. *Modern Ireland 1600-1972*, R.F. Foster, Allen Lane and the Penguin Press, London 1988.

1988. *Mount Eagle*. Collection of Poems by John Montague. Contains the Poem 'The Black Lake', The Gallery Press.

INDEX

Illustration for 'Irish Blessings' by John B. Keane in
Ireland of the Welcomes, vol. 17 no. 4, November–
December 1968. Published by the Irish Tourist Board.